MOM OF 10'S COMPLETE COOKBOOK

Simple Meals for Large Families, Big Crowds, and Busy Nights

Karla Bradley

Table of Contents

📌 Introduction
✔️ Welcome to My Kitchen – How I Feed a Big Family Without Stress
✔️ How to Use This Cookbook – Tips for Navigating the Recipes
✔️ Budget-Friendly & Time-Saving Kitchen Tips

📍 Chapter 1: Instant Pot Favorites (Fast, Set-It-and-Forget-It Meals!)

1. Instant Pot Chicken Alfredo
2. Instant Pot Meatloaf & Mashed Potatoes
3. Instant Pot Potato & Ham Soup
4. Instant Pot Chili
5. Instant Pot Vegetable Soup
6. Instant Pot Salsa Chicken
7. Instant Pot Cheeseburger Soup
8. Instant Pot "Baked" Ziti
9. Instant Pot Chicken, Black Beans & Rice
10. Instant Pot Mississippi Pot Roast
11. Instant Pot Beef Stroganoff
12. Instant Pot Sloppy Joes
13. Instant Pot Honey Garlic Chicken
14. Instant Pot Beef & Broccoli
15. Instant Pot Lasagna Soup

📍 Chapter 2: 30-Minute Meals (Quick & Easy Dinners for Busy Nights!)

1. Creamy Garlic Chicken Pasta
2. One-Pan Chicken Fajitas
3. 15-Minute Shrimp Tacos
4. BBQ Chicken & Cheddar Quesadillas
5. Ground Beef Stir-Fry
6. Baked Marry Me Chicken
7. Sheet Pan Sausage & Veggies
8. Lemon Garlic Butter Salmon
9. Chicken Bacon Ranch Wraps
10. Classic Sloppy Joes
11. Turkey & Cheese Pinwheels
12. Breakfast for Dinner (Pancakes & Scrambled Eggs)
13. Buffalo Chicken Wraps
14. Chicken Caesar Salad
15. Quick Cheesy Taco Pasta

Table of Contents

📍 **Chapter 3: 5-Ingredient Meals**
(Delicious & Simple with Minimal Ingredients!)

1. Instant Pot Mac & Cheese
2. Sheet Pan Sausage & Veggies
3. Pesto Chicken Pasta
4. Honey Garlic Salmon
5. Lemon Butter Chicken
6. Chicken Caesar Wraps
7. Tomato & Mozzarella Flatbread
8. One-Pot Beef & Rice Skillet
9. Garlic Parmesan Zucchini Noodles
10. Ham & Cheese Croissant Sandwiches
11. Caprese Pasta Salad
12. Vegetarian Lentil Soup
13. Greek Yogurt Chicken Salad
14. Baked Potato Bar
15. Spinach & Feta Omelette

📍 **Chapter 4: Meals Under $3 Per Person**
(Stretch Your Grocery Budget Without Sacrificing Flavor!)

1. Instant Pot Lentil Soup
2. Cheesy Potato Casserole
3. Rice & Beans with Sausage
4. Tuna Melt Sandwiches
5. Taco Rice Bowls
6. Spaghetti with Marinara Sauce
7. Baked Ziti
8. Ramen with Egg & Veggies
9. Chicken & Veggie Fried Rice
10. Classic Grilled Cheese & Tomato Soup
11. Slow Cooker Chili
12. Pancakes & Scrambled Eggs
13. Baked Potatoes with Toppings
14. Veggie Stir-Fry with Rice
15, Homemade Sloppy Joes

Table of Contents

📍 **Chapter 5: Crowd-Pleasers**
(Dishes Everyone Loves—Perfect for Big Gatherings!)

1. Instant Pot Lasagna Soup
2. Baked Mac & Cheese
3. Slow Cooker Pulled Pork
4. French Bread Pizza
5. BBQ Chicken Sliders
6. One-Pot Chicken Fajitas
7. Loaded Baked Potatoes
8. Tater Tot Casserole
9. Cheesy Taco Pasta
10. Sourdough Garlic Bread
11. Hawaiian Ham & Cheese Sliders
12. Baked Chicken Parmesan
13. Chicken Enchiladas
14. Buffalo Chicken Dip
15. Sheet Pan Nachos

📍 **Chapter 6: Comfort Food Classics**
(Hearty, Nostalgic, and Oh-So-Satisfying!)

1. Classic Beef Stew
2. Homemade Chicken Pot Pie
3. Meatloaf with Mashed Potatoes
4. Creamy Chicken & Rice Casserole
5. Chicken & Dumplings
6. Classic Chili
7. Biscuits & Sausage Gravy
8. Baked Ziti
9. Pot Roast with Vegetables
10. Homemade Mac & Cheese
11. Shepherd's Pie
12. Chicken Fried Steak with Gravy
13. Slow Cooker Beef Stroganoff
14. Cornbread & Chili
15. Beef & Noodle Casserole

Table of Contents

📍 Chapter 7: Vegetarian Favorites
(Delicious, Meat-Free Options That Everyone Will Love!)

1. Creamy Tomato Basil Soup with Grilled Cheese
2. Vegetarian Chili
3. Caprese Pasta Salad
4. Spinach & Feta Stuffed Peppers
5. Lemon Garlic Butter Salmon
6. Broccoli & Cheese Quiche
7. Vegetable Stir-Fry with Tofu
8. Mushroom Risotto
9. Sweet Potato & Black Bean Tacos
10. Baked Eggplant Parmesan
11. Lentil Soup
12. Zucchini Fritters
13. Garlic Butter Shrimp Pasta
14. Spinach & Ricotta Stuffed Shells
15. Mediterranean Chickpea Salad

📌 Bonus Sections & Resources

✔ Pantry Staples for Large Families – What to Always Keep on Hand
✔ Time-Saving Kitchen Hacks – Smart Tips for Faster Cooking
✔ Money-Saving Grocery Shopping Tips – How to Cut Costs & Plan Smart
✔ Leftover Transformations – Turn Tonight's Meal into Tomorrow's Lunch
✔ Freezer Meal Guide – The Best Meals to Prep & Freeze
✔ Batch Cooking for Large Families – How to Cook Once & Eat Twice

Introduction: Welcome to My Kitchen!

Hi! I'm Karla- a proud mom of 10 who has spent years perfecting the art of feeding a big family without spending a fortune or spending all day in the kitchen.

If you're a busy parent, a home cook looking to streamline meal prep, or someone who loves crowd-pleasing recipes, this book is for you.

Why This Cookbook?

In a household with 10 hungry mouths to feed, I know what it's like to:
✔ Stretch every dollar without sacrificing flavor
✔ Get dinner on the table FAST on busy nights
✔ Find meals that even the pickiest eaters will love
✔ Cook in big batches for leftovers or freezer meals

That's why I created this cookbook—to share my tried-and-true, budget-friendly, and time-saving recipes with other families.

Each recipe in this book is designed to be:
✅ Simple: No fancy ingredients—just pantry staples you already have.
✅ Affordable: Every recipe includes cost-conscious ingredients that won't break the bank.
✅ Family-Approved: Tested by my own family of 10 (so you KNOW they're good).
✅ Fast & Easy: Most meals can be made in 30 minutes or less or in the Instant Pot for busy nights.

How to Use This Cookbook

This book is divided into 7 categories to help you easily find the perfect meal:

📌 Chapter 1: Instant Pot Favorites – Quick, effortless meals using my favorite kitchen gadget.
📌 Chapter 2: 30-Minute Meals – Fast, stress-free meals for busy nights.
📌 Chapter 3: 5-Ingredient Meals – Meals with minimal ingredients but maximum flavor.
📌 Chapter 4: Meals Under $3 Per Person – Budget-friendly meals that won't break the bank.
📌 Chapter 5: Crowd-Pleasers – Dishes perfect for potlucks, gatherings, and feeding a big family.
📌 Chapter 6: Comfort Food Classics – Cozy, nostalgic meals for the whole family.
📌 Chapter 7: Vegetarian Favorites – Delicious, satisfying meals featuring eggs, dairy, and fish.

Whether you're cooking for two or twenty, you'll find meals that are easy, affordable, and guaranteed to please even the pickiest eaters.

I hope this cookbook makes mealtime easier and more enjoyable for you and your family.

Now, let's get cooking!

Happy Cooking,
Karla

📌 Cookbook Organization

To make this book easy to use, here's how each recipe is structured:

❣ Recipe Title – Simple, clear, and family-friendly.
❣ Why You'll Love It – A short description of why this dish is a must-try.
❣ Ingredients List – Includes affordable, easy-to-find ingredients.
❣ Step-by-Step Instructions – Clear, simple, and organized.
❣ Serving Size – Helps you plan for your family's needs.
❣ Make-Ahead & Freezer Tips – For recipes that work well for meal prep.

CHAPTER 1: INSTANT POT MEALS

Introduction to Instant Pot Cooking

Cooking for a large family means I don't have time to spend hours in the kitchen. That's where my Instant Pot comes in! It lets me create flavorful, home-cooked meals in a fraction of the time. Whether you're making comfort food classics or easy weeknight dinners, this chapter is packed with meals that are:

✅ One-pot wonders – Less mess, less cleanup.
✅ Budget-friendly – Stretch ingredients without sacrificing taste.
✅ Time-saving – Most of these meals are ready in under an hour.

1. Instant Pot Chicken Alfredo

Why You'll Love It
This dish is creamy, cheesy, and comforting, and it comes together in under 30 minutes. No need to boil pasta separately—everything cooks right in the Instant Pot!

Ingredients

1 lb boneless, skinless chicken breasts (cubed)

2 cups chicken broth

1 cup heavy cream

8 oz fettuccine pasta (broken in half)

1 cup grated Parmesan cheese

3 cloves garlic (minced)

1 tsp salt

½ tsp black pepper

1 tbsp butter

1 tbsp olive oil

Instructions

1. Sauté the Chicken

Set the Instant Pot to Sauté mode. Add butter and olive oil.

Add cubed chicken and cook for 3–4 minutes until lightly browned.

Stir in garlic, salt, and pepper, cooking for another minute.

2. Cook the Pasta

Pour in the chicken broth and heavy cream. Stir well.

Add broken fettuccine noodles, pressing them down gently into the liquid. (Do NOT stir!)

3. Pressure Cook

Seal the Instant Pot lid and set to High Pressure for 8 minutes.

Once done, do a Quick Release to let out the steam.

4. Make It Creamy

Open the lid and stir in Parmesan cheese. The sauce will thicken as it sits.

Let it rest for 2–3 minutes, then serve hot with extra cheese on top.

2. Instant Pot Meatloaf & Mashed Potatoes

Why You'll Love It

This recipe is a two-in-one meal where you cook juicy meatloaf and creamy mashed potatoes at the same time!

Ingredients

For the Meatloaf:

1 ½ lbs ground beef

½ cup breadcrumbs

1 egg

½ cup milk

2 tbsp ketchup

1 tsp salt

½ tsp black pepper

1 tsp garlic powder

For the Mashed Potatoes:

3 large potatoes (peeled & diced)

½ cup heavy cream

2 tbsp butter

Salt & pepper to taste

Instructions

1. Prepare the Meatloaf

In a bowl, mix together ground beef, breadcrumbs, egg, milk, ketchup, salt, pepper, and garlic powder.

Shape into a loaf and wrap it in aluminum foil.

2. Prep the Potatoes

Place diced potatoes into the bottom of the Instant Pot.

Add 1 cup of water.

3. Cook Everything Together

Place the trivet over the potatoes. Set the wrapped meatloaf on top.

Seal the lid and cook on High Pressure for 25 minutes.

Allow 10 minutes of Natural Release, then Quick Release the rest.

4. Mash the Potatoes

Remove the meatloaf and let it rest. Drain excess water from the potatoes.

Mash the potatoes with butter, heavy cream, salt, and pepper.

5. Serve & Enjoy

Slice the meatloaf and serve with creamy mashed potatoes.

3. Instant Pot Mississippi Pot Roast

Why You'll Love It
This fall-apart tender beef is bursting with savory, tangy flavor. It's only 5 ingredients and is great for feeding a crowd.

Ingredients

3 lb beef chuck roast

1 packet ranch seasoning

1 packet au jus gravy mix

½ cup butter

6 whole pepperoncini peppers

½ cup beef broth

Instructions

1. Sear the Roast

Set Instant Pot to Sauté mode and sear the roast for 3–4 minutes per side.

Turn off sauté mode.

2. Add the Seasonings

Sprinkle the ranch seasoning and au jus mix over the roast.

Place butter and pepperoncini on top.

Pour in beef broth.

3. Pressure Cook

Seal the lid and cook on High Pressure for 60 minutes.

Allow a 15-minute Natural Release.

4. Shred & Serve

Use two forks to shred the beef.

Serve over mashed potatoes, rice, or sandwich buns.

4. Instant Pot Beef Stroganoff

Why You'll Love It:
This creamy, comforting dish features tender beef, rich sauce, and egg noodles, all cooked in one pot. It's a 30-minute meal that feels like Sunday dinner!

Ingredients

1 ½ lbs beef stew meat or sirloin (sliced thin)

1 medium onion (diced)

3 cloves garlic (minced)

2 tbsp butter

2 cups beef broth

1 tbsp Worcestershire sauce

1 tsp salt

½ tsp black pepper

8 oz egg noodles

1 cup sour cream

1 tbsp cornstarch (mixed with 2 tbsp water)

Instructions

1. Sauté the Beef

Set Instant Pot to Sauté mode. Melt butter, then add beef and cook until browned (about 3–4 minutes).

Add onion and garlic; cook another 2 minutes.

2. Add Liquids & Seasonings

Stir in beef broth, Worcestershire sauce, salt, and pepper.

3. Pressure Cook

Seal the lid and set to High Pressure for 12 minutes.

When done, do a Quick Release.

4. Cook the Noodles

Stir in egg noodles and press them down into the liquid.

Seal the lid again and cook on High Pressure for 3 minutes.

Quick Release once done.

5. Make it Creamy

Stir in sour cream and cornstarch slurry to thicken the sauce.

6. Serve & Enjoy

Let rest for 5 minutes, then serve hot!

5. Instant Pot Salsa Chicken

Why You'll Love It:
A super simple, flavorful dish with just 4 ingredients. Perfect for tacos, burritos, or rice bowls!

Ingredients

2 lbs boneless, skinless chicken breasts

1 jar (16 oz) salsa

1 packet taco seasoning

1 cup shredded cheddar cheese

Instructions

1. Add Ingredients to Instant Pot

Place chicken in the pot. Sprinkle taco seasoning over the top.

Pour salsa over everything (don't stir).

2. Pressure Cook

Seal the lid and set to High Pressure for 15 minutes.

Let it naturally release for 5 minutes, then Quick Release the rest.

3. Shred the Chicken

Remove the chicken and shred it with two forks. Return to the pot.

4. Add Cheese & Serve

Stir in cheese until melted.

Serve in tacos, burrito bowls, or over rice.

6. Instant Pot Honey Garlic Chicken

Why You'll Love It:
This sweet & savory dish features tender chicken coated in a garlic honey soy glaze—perfect over rice!

Ingredients

2 lbs chicken thighs (boneless, skinless)

½ cup soy sauce

¼ cup honey

2 cloves garlic (minced)

1 tbsp rice vinegar

1 tbsp cornstarch (mixed with 2 tbsp water)

Instructions

1. Mix Sauce

In a bowl, mix soy sauce, honey, garlic, and vinegar.

2. Pressure Cook

Add chicken to the Instant Pot and pour sauce over it.

Cook on High Pressure for 12 minutes.

Quick Release when done.

3. Thicken Sauce

Turn on Sauté mode and stir in cornstarch slurry.

Let it simmer for 3 minutes until thick.

4. Serve

Spoon chicken over steamed rice and drizzle with sauce.

7. Instant Pot Sloppy Joes

Why You'll Love It:
A kid-friendly classic, ready in 15 minutes! Serve on toasted buns for an easy weeknight dinner.

Ingredients

1 lb ground beef

1 small onion (diced)

1 small bell pepper (diced)

1 can (15 oz) tomato sauce

1 tbsp Worcestershire sauce

1 tbsp brown sugar

1 tsp garlic powder

½ tsp salt

½ tsp black pepper

Instructions

1. Sauté the Beef

Set Instant Pot to Sauté mode. Cook ground beef, onion, and bell pepper for 5 minutes, breaking up the meat.

2. Add Sauce Ingredients

Stir in tomato sauce, Worcestershire sauce, brown sugar, garlic powder, salt, and pepper.

3. Pressure Cook

Seal lid and cook on High Pressure for 5 minutes.

Quick Release when done.

4. Serve

Spoon onto toasted buns and enjoy!

8. Instant Pot "Baked" Ziti

Why You'll Love It:
This no-boil baked ziti is cheesy, saucy, and packed with flavor—without needing the oven! It's a perfect one-pot meal for busy nights.

Ingredients

1 lb ground beef or Italian sausage

1 small onion (diced)

3 cloves garlic (minced)

1 jar (24 oz) marinara sauce

3 cups water

1 box (16 oz) ziti or penne pasta

1 tsp Italian seasoning

½ tsp salt

½ tsp black pepper

1 ½ cups shredded mozzarella cheese

½ cup grated Parmesan cheese

Instructions

1. Sauté the Meat

Set the Instant Pot to Sauté mode. Brown ground beef/sausage with onion for 5 minutes.

Add garlic, Italian seasoning, salt, and pepper. Stir for 1 minute.

2. Add Pasta & Sauce

Pour in marinara sauce and water. Stir well.

Add uncooked pasta, pressing it down into the liquid (do NOT stir).

3. Pressure Cook

Seal lid and set to High Pressure for 6 minutes.

Do a Quick Release once done.

4. Add Cheese & Melt

Stir in Parmesan cheese. Sprinkle mozzarella on top and let it melt.

5. Serve Hot

Let it rest for 5 minutes, then serve!

9. Instant Pot Chili

Why You'll Love It:
This hearty chili is thick, flavorful, and perfect for a crowd. Let the Instant Pot do all the work in under an hour.

Ingredients

1 ½ lbs ground beef

1 small onion (diced)

1 bell pepper (diced)

2 cloves garlic (minced)

1 can (28 oz) crushed tomatoes

1 can (15 oz) black beans (drained)

1 can (15 oz) kidney beans (drained)

2 tbsp chili powder

1 tsp cumin

½ tsp paprika

½ tsp salt

2 cups beef broth

Instructions

1. Sauté the Beef

Set Instant Pot to Sauté mode. Brown ground beef with onion, bell pepper, and garlic for 5 minutes.

Drain excess grease.

2. Add Remaining Ingredients

Stir in crushed tomatoes, beans, beef broth, and seasonings.

3. Pressure Cook

Seal lid and set to High Pressure for 20 minutes.

Allow a 10-minute Natural Release, then Quick Release.

4. Serve Hot

Ladle into bowls and top with shredded cheese, sour cream, and tortilla chips!

10. Instant Pot Beef & Broccoli

Why You'll Love It:
A better-than-takeout meal with tender beef, a rich soy-ginger sauce, and crisp broccoli.

Ingredients

1 ½ lbs flank steak (sliced thin)

1 cup beef broth

¼ cup soy sauce

2 tbsp brown sugar

1 tbsp ginger (grated)

2 cloves garlic (minced)

2 tbsp cornstarch (mixed with 2 tbsp water)

2 cups broccoli florets

1 tbsp sesame seeds (optional)

Instructions

1. Mix the Sauce

In a bowl, mix beef broth, soy sauce, brown sugar, ginger, and garlic.

2. Cook the Beef

Add sliced steak and sauce to the Instant Pot.

Seal lid and cook on High Pressure for 12 minutes.

Quick Release when done.

3. Thicken & Add Broccoli

Stir in cornstarch slurry and broccoli.

Turn on Sauté mode and cook for 3 minutes until thickened.

4. Serve with Rice

Sprinkle with sesame seeds and serve over steamed rice.

11. Instant Pot Chicken & Dumplings

Why You'll Love It:
A comfort food favorite, this dish is creamy, hearty, and filled with tender dumplings.

Ingredients

2 lbs chicken breasts (cubed)

1 small onion (diced)

2 carrots (sliced)

2 celery stalks (sliced)

4 cups chicken broth

1 can (10 oz) cream of chicken soup

1 tsp thyme

1 tsp garlic powder

1 can refrigerated biscuit dough (cut into pieces)

Instructions

1. Sauté the Chicken

Set Instant Pot to Sauté mode. Cook chicken, onion, carrots, and celery for 5 minutes.

2. Add Soup & Seasonings

Stir in chicken broth, cream of chicken soup, thyme, and garlic powder.

3. Pressure Cook

Seal lid and cook on High Pressure for 10 minutes.

Quick Release when done.

4. Add Dumplings & Finish

Stir in biscuit dough pieces and cook on Sauté mode for 5 minutes.

5. Serve Warm

Let it sit for 5 minutes, then enjoy!

12. Instant Pot Cheesy Taco Pasta

Why You'll Love It:
This family-favorite dish combines taco flavors with cheesy pasta in a one-pot meal that's ready in 20 minutes! It's a perfect kid-friendly dinner.

Ingredients

1 lb ground beef

1 small onion (diced)

2 cloves garlic (minced)

1 packet taco seasoning

1 can (10 oz) diced tomatoes with green chilies (Rotel)

3 cups beef broth

12 oz pasta (rotini or shells)

1 ½ cups shredded cheddar cheese

½ cup sour cream

Instructions

1. Sauté the Beef

Set the Instant Pot to Sauté mode.

Cook ground beef and onion for 5 minutes, breaking it apart.

Stir in garlic and cook for 1 more minute.

2. Add Ingredients

Sprinkle in taco seasoning and mix well.

Pour in beef broth, diced tomatoes, and pasta (do NOT stir).

3. Pressure Cook

Seal the lid and set to High Pressure for 5 minutes.

Quick Release when done.

4. Make it Cheesy

Stir in cheddar cheese and sour cream until creamy.

5. Serve & Enjoy

Let sit for 5 minutes before serving. Top with more cheese, salsa, or avocado!

13. Instant Pot Jambalaya

Why You'll Love It:
A flavor-packed, Creole-style dish with rice, sausage, shrimp, and bold spices. Perfect for a crowd or meal prep!

Ingredients

1 tbsp olive oil

12 oz Andouille sausage (sliced)

1 small onion (diced)

1 bell pepper (diced)

2 stalks celery (chopped)

2 cloves garlic (minced)

1 can (14 oz) diced tomatoes

2 cups chicken broth

1 cup long-grain white rice

1 tsp Cajun seasoning

½ tsp thyme

½ tsp paprika

½ tsp black pepper

½ lb shrimp (peeled and deveined)

2 green onions (chopped, for garnish)

Instructions

1. Sauté the Sausage & Vegetables
Set Instant Pot to Sauté mode. Heat olive oil, then brown sausage for 2 minutes.
Add onion, bell pepper, celery, and garlic, cooking for 3 minutes.

2. Add Rice & Seasonings
Stir in diced tomatoes, broth, rice, Cajun seasoning, thyme, paprika, and black pepper.

3. Pressure Cook
Seal the lid and set to High Pressure for 8 minutes.
Quick Release once done.

4. Add Shrimp
Stir in shrimp, then close the lid for 5 minutes to let the shrimp cook in the residual heat.

5. Serve & Enjoy
Fluff with a fork and top with chopped green onions.

14. Instant Pot Lentil Soup

Why You'll Love It:
A hearty, budget-friendly, and protein-packed soup with warm spices and wholesome lentils. This is a perfect meal prep dish that gets better with time!

Ingredients

1 tbsp olive oil

1 small onion (diced)

2 carrots (sliced)

2 stalks celery (chopped)

3 cloves garlic (minced)

1 tsp cumin

½ tsp turmeric

½ tsp paprika

1 cup brown lentils (rinsed)

1 can (14 oz) diced tomatoes

4 cups vegetable broth

1 cup water

½ tsp salt

½ tsp black pepper

1 tbsp lemon juice

Instructions

1. Sauté the Vegetables

Set Instant Pot to Sauté mode. Heat olive oil, then cook onion, carrots, celery, and garlic for 5 minutes.

2. Add Spices & Liquids

Stir in cumin, turmeric, paprika, lentils, diced tomatoes, broth, and water.

3. Pressure Cook

Seal the lid and set to High Pressure for 15 minutes.

Let Natural Release for 10 minutes, then Quick Release.

4. Add Lemon & Serve

Stir in lemon juice, then taste and adjust seasoning.

5. Serve Warm

Enjoy with crusty bread or rice!

15. Instant Pot BBQ Beef Roast

Why You'll Love It:
This fork-tender beef is sweet, smoky, and fall-apart good. Perfect for sandwiches or meal prep!

Ingredients

3 lbs beef chuck roast

1 tbsp olive oil

1 tsp salt

½ tsp black pepper

1 cup beef broth

1 cup BBQ sauce

1 tbsp Worcestershire sauce

1 tbsp apple cider vinegar

½ tsp garlic powder

Instructions

1. Sear the Roast

Set Instant Pot to Sauté mode. Heat olive oil, then sear beef for 3 minutes per side.

2. Add Liquids & Seasonings

Pour in beef broth, BBQ sauce, Worcestershire sauce, apple cider vinegar, and garlic powder.

3. Pressure Cook

Seal the lid and cook on High Pressure for 60 minutes.

Let Natural Release for 15 minutes, then Quick Release.

4. Shred & Serve

Remove roast and shred with two forks. Stir the meat back into the sauce.

5. Serve in Sandwiches or Over Rice

CHAPTER 2: 30-MINUTE MEALS

Introduction to 30-Minute Meals

Between school drop-offs, soccer practice, and never-ending laundry, some nights I need dinner on the table FAST. This chapter is filled with flavorful, homemade meals that are ready in 30 minutes or less—without sacrificing quality or taste.

Each recipe is:
✅ Fast - All done in 30 minutes or less.
✅ Easy - Simple ingredients with minimal prep.
✅ Filling - No one leaves the table hungry!

Let's get cooking!

1. French Bread Pizza

Why You'll Love It:
No rolling dough—just slice French bread in half, load it with toppings, and bake! A fast, easy, and kid-friendly dinner.

Ingredients

1 loaf French bread

1 cup pizza sauce

2 cups shredded mozzarella cheese

½ cup pepperoni slices (or any favorite toppings)

1 tbsp olive oil

1 tsp garlic powder

½ tsp dried oregano

Instructions

1. Preheat the Oven

Set oven to 400°F (200°C).

2. Prepare the Bread

Slice French bread in half lengthwise.

Brush olive oil on each half. Sprinkle garlic powder and oregano.

3. Assemble the Pizza

Spread pizza sauce evenly over the bread.

Sprinkle cheese, then add pepperoni or other toppings.

4. Bake

Place the bread directly on the oven rack for a crispier crust.

Bake for 10–12 minutes, until cheese is melted and bubbly.

5. Slice & Serve

Cut into slices and serve hot!

2. Taco Soup

Why You'll Love It:
A warm, hearty, and flavorful soup that's basically a taco in a bowl!

Ingredients

1 lb ground beef

1 can (15 oz) black beans (drained)

1 can (15 oz) kidney beans (drained)

1 can (15 oz) diced tomatoes

1 cup corn kernels

1 packet taco seasoning

4 cups beef broth

Instructions

1. Cook the Ground Beef

In a large pot, cook ground beef over medium heat until browned.

Drain excess grease.

2. Add Ingredients

Stir in black beans, kidney beans, diced tomatoes, corn, and taco seasoning.

Pour in beef broth and mix well.

3. Simmer

Let it simmer for 15 minutes, stirring occasionally.

4. Serve

Ladle into bowls and top with shredded cheese, sour cream, and tortilla chips!

3. Cheesy Chicken & Rice Casserole

Why You'll Love It:
A one-pan, creamy, cheesy, and filling dinner that's quick and easy.

Ingredients

2 cups cooked chicken (shredded)

1 cup white rice (uncooked)

2 cups chicken broth

1 can (10 oz) cream of chicken soup

1 ½ cups shredded cheddar cheese

½ tsp garlic powder

½ tsp salt

Instructions

1. Preheat the Oven

Set oven to 375°F (190°C).

2. Mix Ingredients

In a baking dish, combine chicken, rice, chicken broth, cream of chicken soup, garlic powder, and salt.

3. Bake

Cover with foil and bake for 25 minutes.

4. Add Cheese & Finish

Remove foil, stir, and sprinkle cheese on top.

Bake 5 more minutes until cheese is melted.

5. Serve & Enjoy

4. Beef Stir-Fry

Why You'll Love It:
A quick and flavorful meal packed with veggies, tender beef, and a delicious sauce.

Ingredients

1 lb thinly sliced beef

1 cup broccoli florets

1 bell pepper (sliced)

1 carrot (julienned)

3 tbsp soy sauce

1 tbsp honey

2 cloves garlic (minced)

1 tbsp cornstarch

1 tbsp vegetable oil

Instructions

1. Marinate the Beef

Mix soy sauce, honey, garlic, and cornstarch. Toss in beef.

2. Cook the Veggies

Heat oil in a pan, stir-fry broccoli, bell pepper, and carrot for 3 minutes.

3. Cook the Beef

Add marinated beef and stir-fry for 5–7 minutes until cooked.

4. Serve Over Rice

5. Baked Tater Tot Casserole

Why You'll Love It:
A family-friendly, cheesy, crispy one-pan meal that's fast, filling, and kid-approved.

Ingredients

1 lb ground beef

1 small onion (diced)

1 can (10 oz) cream of mushroom soup

1 cup sour cream

1 cup shredded cheddar cheese

1 bag (32 oz) frozen tater tots

½ tsp garlic powder

½ tsp salt

½ tsp black pepper

Instructions

1. Preheat Oven

Set to 400°F (200°C).

2. Cook the Beef

In a skillet, brown ground beef and onion over medium heat for 5 minutes.

Drain grease and stir in garlic powder, salt, and pepper.

3. Assemble Casserole

In a baking dish, spread beef mixture evenly.

Stir in cream of mushroom soup and sour cream.

Sprinkle cheddar cheese on top.

4. Add Tater Tots & Bake

Arrange tater tots in a single layer.

Bake for 20 minutes, or until golden brown.

5. Serve Warm

Let rest 5 minutes, then enjoy!

6. Garlic Butter Shrimp Pasta

Why You'll Love It:
A creamy, buttery shrimp dish with tender pasta and garlic-infused sauce.

Ingredients

8 oz linguine or spaghetti

1 lb shrimp (peeled & deveined)

3 tbsp butter

3 cloves garlic (minced)

½ cup heavy cream

¼ cup grated Parmesan cheese

½ tsp salt

¼ tsp black pepper

1 tbsp lemon juice

Instructions

1. Cook the Pasta

Boil pasta in salted water until al dente. Drain.

2. Cook the Shrimp

In a skillet, melt butter over medium heat.

Add garlic and shrimp, cooking for 2-3 minutes per side until pink.

3. Make the Sauce

Reduce heat and stir in heavy cream, Parmesan, salt, and black pepper.

Simmer for 2 minutes.

4. Combine & Serve

Toss pasta in the sauce, squeeze in lemon juice, and serve!

7. Chicken Teriyaki Rice Bowls

Why You'll Love It:
A quick, one-pan meal with sweet and savory teriyaki sauce.

Ingredients

2 cups cooked rice

1 lb chicken breast (diced)

1 cup broccoli florets

1 carrot (julienned)

¼ cup teriyaki sauce

1 tbsp soy sauce

1 tbsp honey

1 tbsp cornstarch (mixed with 2 tbsp water)

Instructions

1. Sauté the Chicken

In a pan, cook chicken over medium heat for 5 minutes.

2. Add Vegetables

Stir in broccoli and carrots, cooking for 3 minutes.

3. Make the Sauce

Mix teriyaki sauce, soy sauce, honey, and cornstarch slurry.

Pour over chicken and simmer for 3 minutes.

4. Serve Over Rice

Spoon mixture over cooked rice and serve hot.

8. Marry Me Chicken

Why You'll Love It:
This creamy, rich chicken dish is so good, it might just earn you a marriage proposal!

Ingredients

2 lbs chicken breasts

1 tbsp olive oil

3 cloves garlic (minced)

½ cup chicken broth

½ cup heavy cream

¼ cup grated Parmesan cheese

1 tsp red pepper flakes

¼ cup sun-dried tomatoes (chopped)

Instructions

1. Sear the Chicken

In a skillet, heat olive oil and cook chicken for 4 minutes per side.

2. Make the Sauce

Stir in garlic, chicken broth, heavy cream, Parmesan, and sun-dried tomatoes.

3. Simmer & Serve

Reduce heat and simmer for 5 minutes.

Serve with pasta or rice.

9. Lemon Chicken

Why You'll Love It:
A bright, fresh chicken dish with zesty lemon sauce. Pairs perfectly with rice, pasta, or roasted veggies!

Ingredients

2 lbs chicken breasts (thinly sliced)

1 tbsp olive oil

1 cup chicken broth

2 tbsp lemon juice

1 tsp lemon zest

2 cloves garlic (minced)

1 tsp salt

½ tsp black pepper

1 tbsp butter

Instructions

1. Sear the Chicken

Heat olive oil in a skillet over medium heat.

Cook chicken breasts for 4 minutes per side until golden brown. Remove from pan.

2. Make the Sauce

In the same pan, melt butter and sauté garlic for 1 minute.

Pour in chicken broth, lemon juice, and lemon zest. Simmer for 2 minutes.

3. Combine & Serve

Return chicken to the pan and simmer for 5 more minutes.

Serve with steamed rice or pasta.

10. Sloppy Joe Sliders

Why You'll Love It:
Mini Sloppy Joes served on Hawaiian rolls—perfect for a quick dinner or party snack!

Ingredients

1 lb ground beef

½ cup ketchup

2 tbsp Worcestershire sauce

1 tbsp brown sugar

1 tsp garlic powder

½ tsp salt

½ tsp black pepper

12 Hawaiian rolls

1 cup shredded cheddar cheese

Instructions

1. Cook the Beef

In a skillet, brown ground beef over medium heat.

Drain grease and stir in ketchup, Worcestershire sauce, brown sugar, garlic powder, salt, and pepper.

2. Simmer & Assemble

Let the mixture simmer for 5 minutes until thickened.

Spoon onto Hawaiian rolls and sprinkle with cheese.

3. Serve Warm

Enjoy immediately with coleslaw or fries!

11. Sheet Pan Chicken Fajitas

Why You'll Love It:
A one-pan meal with tender chicken, colorful bell peppers, and bold fajita seasoning—ready in 20 minutes!

Ingredients

1 ½ lbs chicken breasts (sliced into strips)

3 bell peppers (red, yellow, green, sliced)

1 small onion (sliced)

2 tbsp olive oil

1 packet fajita seasoning

1 tsp lime juice

8 flour tortillas

Instructions

1. Preheat Oven

Set to 400°F (200°C).

2. Season & Bake

Toss chicken, bell peppers, and onion with olive oil and fajita seasoning.

Spread on a baking sheet and bake for 15 minutes, stirring once.

3. Serve

Drizzle with lime juice and serve in warm tortillas!

12. BBQ Chicken Sandwiches

Why You'll Love It:
Shredded BBQ chicken piled high on soft sandwich buns—a quick and easy crowd-pleaser!

Ingredients

2 lbs chicken breasts

1 cup BBQ sauce

½ cup chicken broth

1 tbsp Worcestershire sauce

1 tsp garlic powder

6 sandwich buns

Instructions

1. Cook the Chicken

In a skillet, cook chicken, broth, BBQ sauce, Worcestershire sauce, and garlic powder over medium heat for 15 minutes, covered.

2. Shred & Simmer

Shred chicken with forks and let simmer for 5 minutes.

3. Assemble & Serve

Spoon onto sandwich buns and serve warm!

13. Buffalo Chicken Wraps

Why You'll Love It:
A spicy, crispy, and tangy wrap that's quick and satisfying!

Ingredients

2 cups cooked shredded chicken

¼ cup Buffalo sauce

½ cup ranch dressing

1 cup shredded lettuce

½ cup shredded cheddar cheese

4 flour tortillas

Instructions

1. Warm the Chicken

Toss shredded chicken with Buffalo sauce and heat in a pan for 3 minutes.

2. Assemble Wraps

Lay out tortillas and add lettuce, chicken, cheese, and ranch dressing.

3. Wrap & Serve

Fold and roll tightly. Slice in half and serve!

14. One-Pot Creamy Garlic Noodles

Why You'll Love It:
A cheesy, garlicky pasta dish that's comfort food heaven—and ready in 20 minutes!

Ingredients

8 oz fettuccine or spaghetti

2 tbsp butter

3 cloves garlic (minced)

2 cups chicken broth

1 cup heavy cream

1 cup grated Parmesan cheese

½ tsp salt

½ tsp black pepper

Instructions

1. Sauté Garlic

In a pot, melt butter and sauté garlic for 1 minute.

2. Cook the Pasta

Add chicken broth, cream, salt, and pepper. Bring to a boil.

Stir in pasta and cook for 12 minutes, stirring occasionally.

3. Finish with Cheese

Stir in Parmesan cheese and let thicken for 2 minutes.

4. Serve & Enjoy

Garnish with more cheese or parsley!

15. Cheeseburger Pasta Skillet

Why You'll Love It:
A cheesy, beefy pasta that tastes just like a cheeseburger!

Ingredients

1 lb ground beef

1 small onion (diced)

1 can (14 oz) diced tomatoes

2 cups beef broth

8 oz pasta shells

1 cup shredded cheddar cheese

½ tsp salt

½ tsp black pepper

Instructions

1. Cook the Beef

In a skillet, cook ground beef and onion until browned.

2. Add Pasta & Broth

Stir in diced tomatoes, beef broth, pasta, salt, and pepper.

Simmer for 12 minutes, stirring occasionally.

3. Add Cheese & Serve

Stir in cheese, let melt, then serve warm!

CHAPTER 3: 5-INGREDIENT MEALS

Introduction to 5-Ingredient Meals

Some nights, you just don't have time to deal with a long ingredient list. These 5-ingredient meals are perfect for those busy nights when you need dinner fast but still want something homemade and delicious.

Each recipe in this chapter:
✅ Uses 5 ingredients or fewer
✅ Is budget-friendly
✅ Takes minimal prep and effort

Let's get started!

1. Instant Pot Salsa Chicken

Why You'll Love It:
A dump-and-go meal that's flavor-packed and versatile. Serve it in tacos, burritos, rice bowls, or salads!

Ingredients

2 lbs boneless, skinless chicken breasts

1 jar (16 oz) salsa

1 packet taco seasoning

1 cup shredded cheddar cheese

½ cup sour cream (optional, for serving)

Instructions

1. Add Ingredients to Instant Pot

Place chicken breasts in the Instant Pot.

Sprinkle taco seasoning over the chicken.

Pour salsa on top (do NOT stir).

2. Pressure Cook

Seal the lid and cook on High Pressure for 15 minutes.

Let it naturally release for 5 minutes, then Quick Release.

3. Shred the Chicken

Remove the chicken and shred with two forks. Return to the pot and mix well.

4. Serve

Stir in cheese until melted. Serve in tacos, burritos, or over rice with sour cream!

2. Marry Me Chicken

Why You'll Love It:
This rich, creamy, and flavorful dish comes together with just 5 ingredients and is great over pasta or rice!

Ingredients

2 lbs chicken breasts

½ cup chicken broth

½ cup heavy cream

½ cup grated Parmesan cheese

¼ cup sun-dried tomatoes (chopped)

Instructions

1. Sear the Chicken

In a pan, heat 1 tbsp olive oil over medium heat.

Cook chicken breasts for 4 minutes per side, until golden brown.

2. Make the Sauce

Add chicken broth, heavy cream, Parmesan cheese, and sun-dried tomatoes to the pan.

3. Simmer & Serve

Reduce heat and let simmer for 5 minutes, stirring occasionally.

Serve with pasta or rice.

3. Garlic Butter Shrimp

Why You'll Love It:
This quick and flavorful shrimp dish is perfect over pasta or rice and ready in 10 minutes!

Ingredients

1 lb shrimp (peeled & deveined)

3 tbsp butter

3 cloves garlic (minced)

1 tbsp lemon juice

½ tsp black pepper

Instructions

1. Melt Butter & Sauté Garlic

In a skillet, melt butter over medium heat.

Add garlic and cook for 1 minute until fragrant.

2. Cook the Shrimp

Add shrimp and cook for 2-3 minutes per side, until pink.

3. Finish & Serve

Stir in lemon juice and black pepper.

Serve hot over rice or pasta!

4. BBQ Chicken Sandwiches

Why You'll Love It:
A sweet, smoky, and tangy shredded BBQ chicken sandwich that's great for busy nights.

Ingredients

2 lbs chicken breasts

1 cup BBQ sauce

½ cup chicken broth

1 tbsp Worcestershire sauce

6 sandwich buns

Instructions

1. Cook the Chicken

In a slow cooker or Instant Pot, add chicken, BBQ sauce, chicken broth, and Worcestershire sauce.

2. Slow Cook or Pressure Cook

Slow cooker: Cook on Low for 6 hours or High for 3 hours.

Instant Pot: High Pressure for 15 minutes, Quick Release.

3. Shred & Serve

Shred chicken with forks and return to sauce.

Serve on sandwich buns!

5. Cheesy Baked Tortellini

Why You'll Love It:
A cheesy, bubbly pasta dish with minimal prep and tons of flavor.

Ingredients

1 bag (20 oz) cheese tortellini (refrigerated)

1 jar (24 oz) marinara sauce

1 cup shredded mozzarella cheese

½ cup Parmesan cheese

½ tsp Italian seasoning

Instructions

1. Preheat Oven

Set to 375°F (190°C).

2. Assemble the Dish

In a baking dish, mix tortellini and marinara sauce.

Sprinkle mozzarella and Parmesan cheese on top.

Sprinkle with Italian seasoning.

3. Bake & Serve

Cover with foil and bake for 20 minutes.

Remove foil and bake 5 more minutes until cheese is bubbly.

6. Instant Pot Mac & Cheese

Why You'll Love It:
This creamy, cheesy, and comforting mac & cheese is made in the Instant Pot in just minutes with no draining required!

Ingredients

16 oz elbow macaroni

4 cups water

2 cups shredded cheddar cheese

1 cup heavy cream

½ tsp salt

Instructions

1. Cook the Pasta

Add macaroni, water, and salt to the Instant Pot.

Seal and set to High Pressure for 4 minutes.

Quick Release when done.

2. Make it Creamy

Stir in heavy cream and cheddar cheese until melted and smooth.

3. Serve & Enjoy

Serve immediately while warm and creamy!

7. Sheet Pan Sausage & Veggies

Why You'll Love It:
A healthy, colorful, and flavorful one-pan meal that's easy to prep and clean up!

Ingredients

1 lb smoked sausage (sliced)

2 bell peppers (sliced, any color)

1 small zucchini (sliced)

1 tbsp olive oil

½ tsp Italian seasoning

Instructions

1. Preheat Oven

Set to 400°F (200°C).

2. Season & Bake

Toss sausage and veggies with olive oil and Italian seasoning.

Spread on a baking sheet and bake for 20 minutes, stirring halfway.

3. Serve

Enjoy as is or over rice or pasta!

8. Pesto Chicken Pasta

Why You'll Love It:
A quick and fresh pasta dish with bold pesto flavor and juicy chicken.

Ingredients

12 oz pasta (penne or rotini)

2 cups cooked chicken (shredded or diced)

½ cup pesto sauce

½ cup Parmesan cheese (grated)

1 tbsp olive oil

Instructions

1. Cook the Pasta

Boil pasta in salted water until al dente. Drain.

2. Combine Ingredients

Toss pasta with pesto sauce, chicken, and Parmesan cheese.

3. Serve Warm

Drizzle with olive oil and enjoy!

9. Honey Garlic Salmon

Why You'll Love It:
A sweet and savory salmon dish that's crispy outside, tender inside, and ready in minutes.

Ingredients

4 salmon fillets

2 tbsp honey

2 tbsp soy sauce

2 cloves garlic (minced)

1 tbsp butter

Instructions

1. Make the Glaze

In a bowl, mix honey, soy sauce, and garlic.

2. Sear the Salmon

Heat butter in a skillet over medium heat.

Cook salmon fillets for 3 minutes per side.

3. Glaze & Serve

Pour honey garlic glaze over salmon and cook 1 more minute.

Serve warm with rice or veggies!

10. Lemon Butter Chicken

Why You'll Love It:
A light and zesty chicken dish with buttery lemon sauce that pairs perfectly with rice or pasta.

Ingredients

2 lbs chicken breasts

2 tbsp butter

2 tbsp lemon juice

1 tsp garlic powder

½ tsp salt

Instructions

1. Sear the Chicken

Melt butter in a skillet over medium heat.

Cook chicken for 4 minutes per side.

2. Make the Sauce

Pour in lemon juice, garlic powder, and salt.

Simmer for 2 minutes.

3. Serve

Spoon sauce over chicken and enjoy!

11. Chicken Caesar Wraps

Why You'll Love It:
A quick and fresh wrap with classic Caesar salad flavors and tender chicken.

Ingredients

2 cups cooked chicken (shredded)

½ cup Caesar dressing

1 cup shredded lettuce

½ cup Parmesan cheese

4 flour tortillas

Instructions

1. Mix the Filling

In a bowl, combine chicken, Caesar dressing, lettuce, and Parmesan cheese.

2. Assemble the Wraps

Spoon mixture onto tortillas and roll tightly.

3. Serve & Enjoy

Slice in half and serve!

12. Tomato & Mozzarella Flatbread

Why You'll Love It:
A crispy, cheesy, and flavorful flatbread that's quick to make.

Ingredients

2 flatbreads

½ cup marinara sauce

1 cup shredded mozzarella cheese

½ cup sliced cherry tomatoes

½ tsp Italian seasoning

Instructions

1. Preheat Oven

Set to 400°F (200°C).

2. Assemble & Bake

Spread marinara sauce over flatbreads.

Add mozzarella, tomatoes, and Italian seasoning.

Bake for 10 minutes.

3. Serve Warm

Slice and enjoy!

13. One-Pot Beef & Rice Skillet

Why You'll Love It:
A hearty, one-pan meal with ground beef, rice, and simple spices.

Ingredients

1 lb ground beef

1 cup white rice (uncooked)

2 cups beef broth

1 can (14 oz) diced tomatoes

½ tsp garlic powder

Instructions

1. Cook the Beef

Brown ground beef in a skillet over medium heat.

2. Add Rice & Broth

Stir in rice, beef broth, diced tomatoes, and garlic powder.

Cover and simmer for 15 minutes.

3. Serve

Let rest for 5 minutes, then serve!

14. Garlic Parmesan Zucchini Noodles

Why You'll Love It:
A low-carb alternative to pasta that's light, flavorful, and cheesy!

Ingredients

2 large zucchinis (spiralized)

2 tbsp butter

2 cloves garlic (minced)

½ cup Parmesan cheese

½ tsp black pepper

Instructions

1. Sauté the Garlic

Melt butter in a skillet and cook garlic for 1 minute.

2. Add Zucchini Noodles

Toss in zoodles and cook for 2 minutes.

3. Finish with Parmesan

Stir in cheese and black pepper. Serve warm!

15. Ham & Cheese Croissant Sandwiches

Why You'll Love It:
These warm, buttery, and cheesy croissant sandwiches are simple yet satisfying—perfect for breakfast, lunch, or a quick dinner.

Ingredients

4 croissants (sliced in half)

8 slices ham

4 slices Swiss or cheddar cheese

2 tbsp butter (melted)

1 tsp Dijon mustard (optional)

Instructions

1. Preheat Oven

Set to 375°F (190°C).

2. Assemble the Sandwiches

Spread Dijon mustard on the bottom half of each croissant (if using).

Layer with ham and cheese, then place the top half of the croissant over it.

3. Brush with Butter & Bake

Brush the tops with melted butter.

Place on a baking sheet and bake for 8-10 minutes, until the cheese is melted.

4. Serve Warm

Enjoy immediately with fruit, chips, or a side salad!

Chapter 4: Meals Under $3 Per Person

Introduction to Meals Under $3 Per Person

Feeding a large family on a budget doesn't mean sacrificing flavor or quality. This chapter is filled with affordable, satisfying meals that cost less than $3 per serving while using simple pantry staples.

Each recipe in this chapter:
✅ Uses budget-friendly ingredients
✅ Stretches protein and carbs to feed more people
✅ Takes minimal effort while being filling and delicious

Let's get started!

1. Instant Pot Lentil Soup

Why You'll Love It:
A hearty, protein-packed soup that's incredibly budget-friendly and perfect for meal prep!

Ingredients

1 cup brown lentils (rinsed)

1 can (14 oz) diced tomatoes

4 cups vegetable broth

1 small onion (diced)

2 carrots (chopped)

Instructions

1. Sauté the Onion & Carrots

Set Instant Pot to Sauté mode and cook onions and carrots for 3 minutes.

2. Add Ingredients & Cook

Stir in lentils, diced tomatoes, and vegetable broth.

Seal the lid and cook on High Pressure for 15 minutes.

Let Natural Release for 10 minutes, then Quick Release.

3. Serve & Enjoy

Ladle into bowls and enjoy with crusty bread!

Cost Per Serving: ~$1.50

2. Cheesy Potato Casserole

Why You'll Love It:
This creamy, cheesy, and comforting potato casserole is made with simple, inexpensive ingredients!

Ingredients

4 large potatoes (peeled & diced)

1 can (10 oz) cream of mushroom soup

1 cup shredded cheddar cheese

½ cup sour cream

½ tsp garlic powder

Instructions

1. Preheat Oven

Set to 375°F (190°C).

2. Mix & Assemble

In a large bowl, mix potatoes, soup, sour cream, cheese, and garlic powder.

Spread into a greased baking dish.

3. Bake & Serve

Cover with foil and bake for 35 minutes.

Remove foil and bake for 5 more minutes until golden brown.

Cost Per Serving: ~$2.00

3. Rice & Beans with Sausage

Why You'll Love It:
A simple, protein-packed meal that's affordable, filling, and flavorful.

Ingredients

1 cup white rice

1 can (15 oz) black beans (drained)

1 smoked sausage (sliced)

1 tsp cumin

1 tsp garlic powder

Instructions

1. Cook the Rice

In a pot, cook rice according to package instructions.

2. Sauté the Sausage

In a pan, brown sliced sausage over medium heat.

3. Mix & Serve

Stir in beans, cumin, and garlic powder.

Simmer for 5 minutes and serve over rice.

Cost Per Serving: ~$2.50

4. Tuna Melt Sandwiches

Why You'll Love It:
A quick, easy, and inexpensive sandwich made with pantry staples!

Ingredients

2 cans (5 oz each) tuna (drained)

½ cup mayonnaise

1 tsp mustard

4 slices cheese (cheddar or Swiss)

8 slices bread

Instructions

1. Make the Tuna Salad

Mix tuna, mayo, and mustard in a bowl.

2. Assemble Sandwiches

Spread tuna mixture onto 4 slices of bread.

Add a slice of cheese and top with another slice of bread.

3. Toast & Serve

Toast in a pan for 3 minutes per side, until golden brown.

Cost Per Serving: ~$2.75

5. Taco Rice Bowls

Why You'll Love It:
A quick and easy Mexican-inspired meal that's filling and affordable!

Ingredients

1 lb ground beef or turkey

1 packet taco seasoning

1 can (15 oz) black beans (drained)

2 cups cooked rice

½ cup shredded cheese

Instructions

1. Cook the Meat

In a pan, brown ground beef and drain grease.

Stir in taco seasoning and black beans.

2. Assemble Bowls

Scoop cooked rice into bowls.

Top with taco meat and shredded cheese.

3. Serve & Enjoy

Add toppings like sour cream, salsa, or avocado if available!

Cost Per Serving: ~$2.50

6. Spaghetti with Marinara Sauce

Why You'll Love It:
A simple, comforting Italian meal made with just a few pantry staples!

Ingredients

12 oz spaghetti

1 jar (24 oz) marinara sauce

1 tbsp olive oil

2 cloves garlic (minced)

½ tsp salt

Instructions

1. Cook the Spaghetti

Boil water in a large pot, add spaghetti, and cook according to package directions. Drain.

2. Prepare the Sauce

Heat olive oil in a pan and sauté garlic for 1 minute.

Pour in marinara sauce and simmer for 5 minutes.

3. Combine & Serve

Toss cooked spaghetti with marinara sauce and season with salt.

Serve warm with grated Parmesan (optional).

Cost Per Serving: ~$2.00

7. Baked Ziti

Why You'll Love It:
A cheesy, filling pasta dish that's affordable and perfect for leftovers.

Ingredients

12 oz ziti or penne pasta

1 jar (24 oz) marinara sauce

1 cup shredded mozzarella cheese

½ cup Parmesan cheese

½ tsp Italian seasoning

Instructions

1. Preheat Oven

Set to 375°F (190°C).

2. Cook Pasta & Mix

Boil pasta until al dente, then drain.

Mix with marinara sauce and spread in a baking dish.

3. Add Cheese & Bake

Sprinkle mozzarella and Parmesan cheese on top.

Bake for 20 minutes until cheese is bubbly.

4. Serve Warm

Garnish with Italian seasoning and enjoy!

Cost Per Serving: ~$2.50

8. Ramen with Egg & Veggies

Why You'll Love It:
An upgraded version of instant ramen that's cheap but satisfying!

Ingredients

2 packs instant ramen (any flavor)

2 eggs (soft-boiled or scrambled)

1 cup frozen mixed vegetables

1 tbsp soy sauce

1 tsp sesame oil (optional)

Instructions

1. Cook the Ramen

Boil ramen noodles according to package instructions. Drain half the water.

2. Add Veggies & Flavor

Stir in frozen veggies, soy sauce, and seasoning packet.

3. Add the Egg

Crack an egg into the hot soup and stir for 30 seconds, or top with a soft-boiled egg.

4. Serve Warm

Drizzle with sesame oil for extra flavor.

Cost Per Serving: ~$1.75

9. Chicken & Veggie Fried Rice

Why You'll Love It:
A quick, budget-friendly way to use up leftover rice with simple, flavorful ingredients.

Ingredients

2 cups cooked rice (day-old works best)

1 cup cooked chicken (diced)

1 cup frozen mixed vegetables

2 tbsp soy sauce

1 egg (scrambled)

Instructions

1. Scramble the Egg

In a pan, cook scrambled egg and set aside.

2. Cook the Veggies & Chicken

In the same pan, heat cooked chicken and mixed vegetables for 3 minutes.

3. Stir-Fry Everything

Add cooked rice, soy sauce, and scrambled egg.

Stir-fry for 5 minutes until heated through.

4. Serve Warm

Enjoy as is or with sriracha for extra spice!

Cost Per Serving: ~$2.50

10. Classic Grilled Cheese & Tomato Soup

Why You'll Love It:
A warm, comforting meal that's simple, cheap, and delicious.

Ingredients

8 slices bread

4 slices cheddar cheese

2 tbsp butter

1 can (14 oz) tomato soup

½ cup milk

Instructions

1. Make the Soup

Heat tomato soup and milk in a pot over low heat.

2. Grill the Cheese Sandwiches

Spread butter on bread slices, add cheese, and grill in a pan for 3 minutes per side.

3. Serve Warm

Enjoy with a hot bowl of tomato soup!

Cost Per Serving: ~$2.75

11. Slow Cooker Chili

Why You'll Love It:
A big pot of hearty chili that's affordable and perfect for leftovers.

Ingredients

1 lb ground beef

1 can (15 oz) kidney beans

1 can (15 oz) black beans

1 can (28 oz) crushed tomatoes

1 tbsp chili powder

Instructions

1. Brown the Beef

In a pan, cook ground beef until browned. Drain grease.

2. Slow Cook

Add beef, beans, tomatoes, and chili powder to a slow cooker.

Cook on Low for 6 hours or High for 3 hours.

3. Serve Hot

Enjoy with bread or rice!

Cost Per Serving: ~$2.50

2. Pancakes & Scrambled Eggs

Why You'll Love It:
A quick, filling, and cheap breakfast-for-dinner meal!

Ingredients

2 cups pancake mix

1 cup milk

2 eggs (for pancakes)

2 eggs (scrambled separately)

1 tbsp butter

Instructions

1. Make the Pancakes

Mix pancake batter and cook on a griddle.

2. Scramble the Eggs

In a pan, cook scrambled eggs with butter.

3. Serve Warm

Stack pancakes, add butter & syrup, and serve with eggs.

Cost Per Serving: ~$2.00

13. Baked Potatoes with Toppings

Why You'll Love It:
A customizable, affordable meal with simple pantry ingredients.

Ingredients

4 large potatoes

1 cup shredded cheese

½ cup sour cream

½ cup butter

½ tsp salt

Instructions

1. Bake the Potatoes

Pierce with a fork and bake at 400°F (200°C) for 50 minutes.

2. Add Toppings

Split open and top with butter, cheese, and sour cream.

Cost Per Serving: ~$2.25

14. Veggie Stir-Fry with Rice

Why You'll Love It:
A healthy, colorful, and affordable meal that's quick to make and easy to customize with whatever veggies you have on hand.

Ingredients

2 cups cooked rice

2 cups mixed vegetables (fresh or frozen)

2 tbsp soy sauce

1 tbsp vegetable oil

1 tsp garlic powder

Instructions

1. Prepare the Rice

Cook rice according to package instructions.

2. Stir-Fry the Veggies

Heat vegetable oil in a pan over medium-high heat.

Add vegetables and stir-fry for 5 minutes until tender.

3. Add Seasoning & Serve

Stir in garlic powder and soy sauce.

Serve hot over steamed rice.

Cost Per Serving: ~$2.00

15. Homemade Sloppy Joes

Why You'll Love It:
A hearty, comforting meal that's budget-friendly and feeds a crowd!

Ingredients

1 lb ground beef

½ cup ketchup

1 tbsp Worcestershire sauce

½ tsp garlic powder

4 hamburger buns

Instructions

1. Cook the Beef

In a skillet, brown ground beef over medium heat for 5 minutes. Drain excess grease.

2. Make the Sauce

Stir in ketchup, Worcestershire sauce, and garlic powder.

Simmer for 5 minutes, stirring occasionally.

3. Assemble & Serve

Spoon mixture onto hamburger buns and serve warm.

Cost Per Serving: ~$2.50

CHAPTER 5: CROWD-PLEASERS

Introduction to Crowd-Pleasers

When you're feeding a big family or hosting a gathering, you need meals that are filling, easy to prepare, and loved by everyone. These recipes are budget-friendly, make large portions, and can be prepped ahead of time to keep everyone happy and well-fed.

Each recipe in this chapter:
- ✅ Makes generous portions
- ✅ Uses simple, affordable ingredients
- ✅ Is family-approved and potluck-friendly

Let's get started!

1. Instant Pot Lasagna Soup

Why You'll Love It:
All the cheesy, saucy goodness of lasagna in a quick and easy soup format!

Ingredients

1 lb ground beef or Italian sausage

1 small onion (diced)

3 cloves garlic (minced)

4 cups chicken or beef broth

1 can (28 oz) crushed tomatoes

8 lasagna noodles (broken into pieces)

1 tsp Italian seasoning

½ tsp salt

½ tsp black pepper

1 cup shredded mozzarella cheese

½ cup ricotta cheese

Instructions

1. Sauté the Meat & Aromatics

Set Instant Pot to Sauté mode. Brown ground beef, then add onion and garlic. Cook for 3 minutes.

2. Add Liquids & Noodles

Pour in broth, crushed tomatoes, Italian seasoning, salt, and pepper.

Stir in broken lasagna noodles.

3. Pressure Cook

Seal lid and set to High Pressure for 6 minutes.

Quick Release once done.

4. Add Cheese & Serve

Stir in mozzarella cheese and dollop with ricotta cheese.

Serves: 6-8

2. Baked Mac & Cheese

Why You'll Love It:
A classic comfort food that's creamy, cheesy, and perfect for feeding a crowd.

Ingredients

16 oz elbow macaroni

4 cups shredded cheddar cheese

2 cups milk

1 can (10 oz) cream of cheddar soup

1 tsp salt

Instructions

1. Cook the Pasta

Boil macaroni until al dente. Drain.

2. Mix & Bake

Stir together macaroni, 3 cups cheese, milk, soup, and salt in a baking dish.

Top with remaining cheese.

3. Bake & Serve

Bake at 375°F for 20 minutes until golden brown.

Serves: 8-10

3. Slow Cooker Pulled Pork

Why You'll Love It:
A set-it-and-forget-it meal that makes tender, juicy pulled pork—perfect for sandwiches or tacos.

Ingredients

3 lb pork shoulder

1 cup BBQ sauce

½ cup chicken broth

1 tbsp Worcestershire sauce

1 tsp garlic powder

Instructions

1. Prepare the Pork

Place pork shoulder in a slow cooker.

Pour in broth, BBQ sauce, Worcestershire sauce, and garlic powder.

2. Slow Cook

Cook on Low for 8 hours or High for 4 hours.

3. Shred & Serve

Shred pork with forks and mix back into the sauce.

Serve on buns or tortillas!

Serves: 8-10

4. French Bread Pizza

Why You'll Love It:
An easy, customizable meal that's great for feeding a large group without much effort.

Ingredients

2 French bread loaves

2 cups pizza sauce

3 cups shredded mozzarella cheese

½ cup pepperoni slices (or any toppings)

1 tsp Italian seasoning

Instructions

1. Preheat Oven

Set to 400°F (200°C).

2. Assemble the Pizza

Slice French bread in half lengthwise.

Spread with pizza sauce and top with cheese and pepperoni.

3. Bake & Serve

Bake for 10 minutes until cheese is bubbly.

Serves: 8

5. BBQ Chicken Sliders

Why You'll Love It:
These mini BBQ sandwiches are sweet, smoky, and packed with flavor—perfect for a crowd!

Ingredients

2 lbs boneless, skinless chicken breasts

1 cup BBQ sauce

½ cup chicken broth

12 Hawaiian slider rolls

½ cup shredded cheddar cheese

Instructions

1. Slow Cook the Chicken

Place chicken, BBQ sauce, and chicken broth in a slow cooker.

Cook on Low for 6 hours or High for 3 hours.

2. Shred the Chicken

Shred chicken with forks and mix into sauce.

3. Assemble Sliders

Slice slider rolls in half, add BBQ chicken and cheese, and top with the other half.

4. Serve & Enjoy

Enjoy warm, optionally baked for 5 minutes at 350°F for melty cheese.

Serves: 8-10

6. One-Pot Chicken Fajitas

Why You'll Love It:
A quick and easy meal with tender chicken, colorful bell peppers, and bold seasoning—perfect for tacos or bowls!

Ingredients

2 lbs chicken breasts (sliced into strips)

3 bell peppers (sliced, any color)

1 small onion (sliced)

1 packet fajita seasoning

1 tbsp olive oil

Instructions

1. Cook the Chicken

Heat olive oil in a large skillet.

Add chicken and cook for 5 minutes, stirring occasionally.

2. Add Peppers & Seasoning

Stir in peppers, onion, and fajita seasoning.

Cook for 5 more minutes until tender.

3. Serve

Enjoy in flour tortillas with toppings like sour cream and cheese!

Serves: 6-8

7. Loaded Baked Potatoes

Why You'll Love It:
A customizable, filling meal where everyone chooses their own toppings!

Ingredients

6 large potatoes

1 cup shredded cheddar cheese

1 cup sour cream

½ cup cooked bacon crumbles

2 tbsp butter

Instructions

1. Bake the Potatoes

Preheat oven to 400°F (200°C).

Pierce potatoes with a fork and bake for 1 hour.

2. Prepare Toppings

Arrange cheese, sour cream, bacon, and butter for serving.

3. Assemble & Serve

Split potatoes open and top with desired toppings.

Serves: 6

8. Tater Tot Casserole

Why You'll Love It:
A cheesy, beefy, potato-filled dish that's easy and comforting for a big group.

Ingredients

1 lb ground beef

1 can (10 oz) cream of mushroom soup

1 cup shredded cheddar cheese

1 bag (32 oz) frozen tater tots

½ tsp garlic powder

Instructions

1. Cook the Beef

In a skillet, cook ground beef until browned. Drain excess grease.

2. Assemble the Casserole

In a baking dish, mix beef, soup, and garlic powder.

Sprinkle cheese on top, then layer tater tots.

3. Bake & Serve

Bake at 375°F for 30 minutes until golden brown.

Serves: 8-10

9. Cheesy Taco Pasta

Why You'll Love It:
A kid-friendly pasta dish with taco flavors and lots of cheese!

Ingredients

1 lb ground beef

1 packet taco seasoning

12 oz pasta (rotini or shells)

2 cups beef broth

1 ½ cups shredded cheddar cheese

Instructions

1. Cook the Beef

Brown ground beef in a skillet, then drain.

2. Cook the Pasta

Add pasta, taco seasoning, and beef broth.

Simmer for 12 minutes, stirring occasionally.

3. Add Cheese & Serve

Stir in cheddar cheese until melted.

Serves: 6-8

10. Sourdough Garlic Bread

Why You'll Love It:
A crispy, garlicky side that pairs perfectly with pasta or soups.

Ingredients

1 sourdough loaf

4 tbsp butter (melted)

3 cloves garlic (minced)

½ tsp Italian seasoning

¼ cup Parmesan cheese

Instructions

1. Preheat Oven

Set to 375°F (190°C).

2. Prepare the Bread

Slice sourdough loaf and spread with garlic butter.

Sprinkle with Italian seasoning and Parmesan.

3. Bake & Serve

Bake for 10 minutes, then broil for 2 minutes for crispiness.

Serves: 8

11. Hawaiian Ham & Cheese Sliders

Why You'll Love It:
These sweet, savory, and cheesy mini sandwiches are a hit at parties, potlucks, or family dinners.

Ingredients

12 Hawaiian slider rolls

1/2 lb sliced ham

6 slices Swiss or cheddar cheese

4 tbsp butter (melted)

1 tbsp Dijon mustard

1 tbsp poppy seeds (optional for topping)

Instructions

1. Preheat Oven

Set oven to 350°F (175°C).

2. Assemble the Sliders

Slice Hawaiian rolls in half and place the bottom half in a baking dish.

Layer with ham and cheese, then top with the other half of the rolls.

3. Make the Butter Glaze

Mix melted butter, Dijon mustard, and poppy seeds.

Brush over the tops of the sliders.

4. Bake & Serve

Cover with foil and bake for 10 minutes.

Remove foil and bake for 5 more minutes, until golden brown.

Serves: 6-8

12. Baked Chicken Parmesan

Why You'll Love It:
A crispy, cheesy, and saucy Italian favorite that's easy to make for a crowd!

Ingredients

4 boneless, skinless chicken breasts

1 cup breadcrumbs

1/2 cup Parmesan cheese (grated)

2 cups marinara sauce

1 cup shredded mozzarella cheese

Instructions

1. Preheat Oven

Set to 375°F (190°C).

2. Bread the Chicken

Mix breadcrumbs and Parmesan cheese.

Coat each chicken breast in the breadcrumb mixture.

3. Bake the Chicken

Place chicken in a greased baking dish.

Bake for 20 minutes, then flip and bake 10 more minutes.

4. Add Sauce & Cheese

Spoon marinara sauce over each chicken breast.

Sprinkle with mozzarella cheese.

5. Bake & Serve

Return to oven for 5 minutes, until cheese is melted and bubbly.

Serves: 6

13. Chicken Enchiladas

Why You'll Love It:
These cheesy, saucy, and satisfying enchiladas are easy to make and perfect for feeding a large family.

Ingredients

2 cups cooked shredded chicken

8 flour tortillas

2 cups enchilada sauce

1 ½ cups shredded cheese (cheddar or Mexican blend)

½ tsp cumin

Instructions

1. Preheat Oven

Set to 375°F (190°C).

2. Fill & Roll the Tortillas

Mix chicken and cumin.

Spoon chicken into each tortilla, add a little cheese, and roll up.

3. Assemble the Dish

Place rolled enchiladas seam-side down in a baking dish.

Pour enchilada sauce over the top and sprinkle with cheese.

4. Bake & Serve

Cover with foil and bake for 20 minutes.

Remove foil and bake for 5 more minutes, until cheese is bubbly.

Serves: 6-8

14. Buffalo Chicken Dip

Why You'll Love It:
This creamy, cheesy, spicy dip is perfect for game days, potlucks, and parties!

Ingredients

2 cups cooked shredded chicken

8 oz cream cheese (softened)

½ cup Buffalo sauce

½ cup ranch dressing

1 cup shredded cheddar cheese

Instructions

1. Preheat Oven

Set to 350°F (175°C).

2. Mix the Dip

In a bowl, mix chicken, cream cheese, Buffalo sauce, and ranch dressing.

3. Assemble & Bake

Spread mixture in a baking dish and top with cheddar cheese.

Bake for 20 minutes, until bubbly.

4. Serve Warm

Serve with tortilla chips, celery, or crackers!

Serves: 8-10

15. Sheet Pan Nachos

Why You'll Love It:
An easy, shareable meal loaded with cheese, seasoned beef, and toppings!

Ingredients

1 bag (12 oz) tortilla chips

1 lb ground beef

1 packet taco seasoning

2 cups shredded cheese (cheddar or Mexican blend)

½ cup salsa

Instructions

1. Preheat Oven

Set to 375°F (190°C).

2. Cook the Beef

Brown ground beef in a pan, then drain.

Stir in taco seasoning and cook for 2 more minutes.

3. Assemble the Nachos

Spread tortilla chips on a baking sheet.

Top with beef and shredded cheese.

4. Bake & Serve

Bake for 10 minutes, until cheese is melted.

Serve with salsa, sour cream, or guacamole!

Serves: 8-10

CHAPTER 6: COMFORT FOOD CLASSICS

Introduction to Comfort Food Classics

Some nights call for good old-fashioned comfort food—the kind of meals that bring back childhood memories, warm your soul, and fill your belly. These dishes are rich, flavorful, and satisfying, making them perfect for family dinners, cozy nights in, or special occasions.

Each recipe in this chapter:
✅ Features classic, home-cooked flavors
✅ Uses simple, pantry-friendly ingredients
✅ Is filling and satisfying for the whole family

Let's dive into these cozy, delicious meals!

1. Classic Beef Stew

Why You'll Love It:
A hearty, slow-cooked stew with tender beef, carrots, and potatoes—the ultimate comfort meal!

Ingredients

2 lbs beef chuck (cubed)

4 cups beef broth

3 potatoes (peeled & chopped)

3 carrots (sliced)

1 small onion (diced)

2 cloves garlic (minced)

1 tbsp tomato paste

1 tsp thyme

1 tbsp flour (for thickening, optional)

1 tbsp olive oil

Salt & pepper to taste

Instructions

1. Sear the Beef

Heat olive oil in a large pot.

Add beef cubes, season with salt and pepper, and brown on all sides.

2. Add Aromatics & Broth

Stir in onion, garlic, carrots, and potatoes.

Add tomato paste, thyme, and beef broth.

3. Simmer & Thicken

Cover and simmer for 2 hours, stirring occasionally.

If desired, mix flour with 2 tbsp water and stir in to thicken.

4. Serve Hot

Ladle into bowls and serve with crusty bread!

Serves: 6-8

2. Homemade Chicken Pot Pie

Why You'll Love It:
A flaky, golden crust filled with creamy chicken and vegetables—a true comfort food classic!

Ingredients

2 cups cooked, shredded chicken

1 cup chicken broth

1 cup heavy cream

2 cups mixed vegetables (peas, carrots, corn)

2 tbsp butter

1 tsp garlic powder

2 pie crusts (store-bought or homemade)

Instructions

1. Preheat Oven

Set to 375°F (190°C).

2. Make the Filling

In a pan, melt butter and stir in vegetables and garlic powder.

Pour in broth and cream, then mix in chicken.

3. Assemble the Pie

Roll out one pie crust in a greased pie dish.

Pour in chicken mixture, then cover with the second pie crust.

Seal edges and cut small slits in the top.

4. Bake & Serve

Bake for 35-40 minutes, until golden brown.

Serves: 6-8

3. Meatloaf with Mashed Potatoes

Why You'll Love It:
A classic American comfort food that's juicy, flavorful, and pairs perfectly with mashed potatoes!

Ingredients

1 ½ lbs ground beef

½ cup breadcrumbs

1 egg

½ cup milk

½ cup ketchup

1 tsp garlic powder

1 tsp salt

½ tsp black pepper

Instructions

1. Preheat Oven

Set to 375°F (190°C).

2. Prepare the Meatloaf

In a bowl, mix ground beef, breadcrumbs, egg, milk, ketchup, garlic powder, salt, and pepper.

Shape into a loaf and place in a greased baking dish.

3. Bake & Serve

Bake for 45 minutes, then let rest for 10 minutes before slicing.

Serve with mashed potatoes and gravy.

Serves: 6-8

4. Creamy Chicken & Rice Casserole

Why You'll Love It:
A one-pan, creamy, cheesy chicken and rice dish that's easy and comforting!

Ingredients

2 cups cooked, shredded chicken

1 cup white rice (uncooked)

2 cups chicken broth

1 can (10 oz) cream of chicken soup

1 ½ cups shredded cheddar cheese

Instructions

1. Preheat Oven

Set to 375°F (190°C).

2. Mix Ingredients

In a baking dish, combine chicken, rice, chicken broth, cream of chicken soup, and half the cheese.

3. Bake & Finish

Cover with foil and bake for 25 minutes.

Remove foil, stir, and sprinkle with remaining cheese.

4. Bake & Serve

Bake 5 more minutes, until cheese is melted.

Serves: 6

5. Chicken & Dumplings

Why You'll Love It:
A cozy, creamy dish with fluffy dumplings floating in a rich, savory broth—this is a true Southern classic!

Ingredients

2 cups cooked, shredded chicken

4 cups chicken broth

1 cup heavy cream

1 cup frozen peas and carrots

1 tsp thyme

2 cups biscuit mix (like Bisquick)

⅔ cup milk

Instructions

1. Simmer the Soup

In a pot, bring chicken broth, shredded chicken, peas and carrots, cream, and thyme to a simmer.

2. Make the Dumplings

In a bowl, mix biscuit mix and milk until combined.

3. Drop in Dumplings

Drop spoonfuls of dough into the pot, cover, and let cook for 15 minutes.

4. Serve Hot

Ladle into bowls and enjoy!

Serves: 6

6. Classic Chili

Why You'll Love It:
A rich, slow-cooked beef and bean chili that's thick, hearty, and packed with flavor!

Ingredients

1 lb ground beef

1 small onion (diced)

1 can (15 oz) kidney beans (drained)

1 can (15 oz) black beans (drained)

1 can (28 oz) crushed tomatoes

2 tbsp chili powder

1 tsp cumin

½ tsp garlic powder

½ tsp salt

Instructions

1. Sauté the Beef

In a pot, brown ground beef and onion for 5 minutes.

2. Add Ingredients & Simmer

Stir in beans, tomatoes, chili powder, cumin, garlic powder, and salt.

Simmer for 30 minutes, stirring occasionally.

3. Serve Warm

Ladle into bowls and top with cheese, sour cream, or cornbread.

Serves: 6-8

7. Biscuits & Sausage Gravy

Why You'll Love It:
A Southern breakfast classic with flaky biscuits smothered in creamy sausage gravy.

Ingredients

8 biscuits (store-bought or homemade)

1 lb breakfast sausage

2 cups milk

2 tbsp flour

½ tsp black pepper

Instructions

1. Bake the Biscuits

Follow package instructions or bake homemade biscuits.

2. Make the Sausage Gravy

In a pan, cook sausage until browned.

Sprinkle flour over sausage and stir for 1 minute.

Pour in milk, whisking constantly, and cook for 5 minutes, until thickened.

Season with black pepper.

3. Serve Hot

Spoon sausage gravy over warm biscuits.

Serves: 6

8. Baked Ziti

Why You'll Love It:
A cheesy, oven-baked pasta dish that's perfect for feeding a crowd.

Ingredients

12 oz ziti or penne pasta

1 jar (24 oz) marinara sauce

1 lb ground beef or Italian sausage

2 cups shredded mozzarella cheese

½ cup Parmesan cheese

Instructions

1. Preheat Oven

Set to 375°F (190°C).

2. Cook Pasta & Meat

Boil pasta until al dente. Drain.

Brown ground beef, then mix with marinara sauce.

3. Assemble & Bake

In a baking dish, layer pasta, meat sauce, mozzarella, and Parmesan cheese.

Bake for 25 minutes, until bubbly.

Serves: 6-8

9. Pot Roast with Vegetables

Why You'll Love It:
A fall-apart tender beef roast with flavorful carrots and potatoes, slow-cooked to perfection!

Ingredients

3 lb beef chuck roast

4 cups beef broth

3 potatoes (cut into chunks)

3 carrots (sliced)

1 small onion (diced)

2 cloves garlic (minced)

1 tsp rosemary

½ tsp black pepper

Instructions

1. Sear the Roast

In a pan, sear roast on all sides for 3 minutes per side.

2. Slow Cook

Place roast, broth, potatoes, carrots, onion, garlic, rosemary, and pepper in a slow cooker.

Cook on Low for 8 hours or High for 4 hours.

3. Serve Hot

Slice and serve with vegetables.

Serves: 6-8

10. Homemade Mac & Cheese

Why You'll Love It:
This rich, creamy, and cheesy mac & cheese is baked to golden perfection, making it the ultimate comfort food favorite!

Ingredients

16 oz elbow macaroni

4 tbsp butter

¼ cup flour

3 cups milk

3 cups shredded cheddar cheese

½ tsp salt

½ tsp black pepper

Instructions

1. Preheat Oven

Set to 375°F (190°C).

2. Cook the Pasta

Boil macaroni in salted water until al dente. Drain.

3. Make the Cheese Sauce

In a saucepan, melt butter and whisk in flour for 1 minute.

Slowly whisk in milk, stirring until thickened.

Add cheddar cheese, salt, and black pepper. Stir until melted.

4. Assemble & Bake

Combine cooked pasta and cheese sauce in a baking dish.

Bake for 20 minutes, until bubbly and golden brown.

Serves: 6-8

11. Shepherd's Pie

Why You'll Love It:
This classic British dish is a savory, hearty casserole with flavorful ground beef, vegetables, and a fluffy mashed potato topping!

Ingredients

1 lb ground beef

1 small onion (diced)

1 cup frozen peas & carrots

1 tbsp tomato paste

1 tsp Worcestershire sauce

2 cups mashed potatoes

½ cup shredded cheddar cheese

Instructions

1. Preheat Oven

Set to 375°F (190°C).

2. Cook the Beef & Vegetables

In a skillet, brown ground beef and onion. Drain grease.

Stir in peas, carrots, tomato paste, and Worcestershire sauce.

3. Assemble the Dish

Spread the beef mixture into a baking dish.

Top with mashed potatoes and sprinkle with cheddar cheese.

4. Bake & Serve

Bake for 25 minutes, until golden brown.

Serves: 6

12. Chicken Fried Steak with Gravy

Why You'll Love It:
A crispy, golden-fried steak smothered in a creamy, peppered gravy—a true Southern classic!

Ingredients

4 cube steaks

1 cup flour

1 tsp salt

1 tsp black pepper

2 cups milk

2 tbsp butter

1 cup vegetable oil (for frying)

Instructions

1. Prepare the Breading

In a bowl, mix flour, salt, and pepper.

Dredge each cube steak in the flour mixture, coating well.

2. Fry the Steaks

Heat vegetable oil in a pan over medium-high heat.

Fry steaks for 3-4 minutes per side, until crispy. Drain on paper towels.

3. Make the Gravy

In the same pan, melt butter, then whisk in 2 tbsp flour from the breading mixture.

Slowly pour in milk, whisking constantly, until thickened.

4. Serve & Enjoy

Pour gravy over fried steak and serve with mashed potatoes.

Serves: 4-6

13. Slow Cooker Beef Stroganoff

Why You'll Love It:
A creamy, beef and mushroom dish slow-cooked to tender perfection, served over egg noodles.

Ingredients

2 lbs beef stew meat (cubed)

1 small onion (diced)

1 cup sliced mushrooms

2 cups beef broth

1 tbsp Worcestershire sauce

1 cup sour cream

12 oz egg noodles

Instructions

1. Slow Cook the Beef

In a slow cooker, add beef, onion, mushrooms, broth, and Worcestershire sauce.

Cook on Low for 6-8 hours or High for 4 hours.

2. Cook the Noodles

Boil egg noodles and drain.

3. Add Sour Cream & Serve

Stir sour cream into the slow cooker just before serving.

Serve over egg noodles.

Serves: 6-8

14. Cornbread & Chili

Why You'll Love It:
A warm, buttery cornbread pairs perfectly with a hearty chili for the ultimate comfort meal.

Ingredients for Cornbread

1 cup cornmeal

1 cup flour

1 tbsp baking powder

½ tsp salt

1 cup milk

1 egg

¼ cup butter (melted)

Ingredients for Chili

1 lb ground beef

1 can (15 oz) kidney beans

1 can (15 oz) black beans

1 can (28 oz) crushed tomatoes

1 tbsp chili powder

Instructions

Make the Cornbread

1. Preheat Oven

Set to 375°F (190°C).

2. Mix & Bake

Mix all cornbread ingredients in a bowl.

Pour into a greased baking dish and bake for 20 minutes.

Make the Chili

1. Cook the Beef

Brown ground beef in a pot. Drain grease.

2. Add Ingredients & Simmer

Stir in beans, tomatoes, and chili powder.

Simmer for 30 minutes.

3. Serve Together

Slice cornbread and serve with a bowl of chili.

Serves: 6-8

15. Beef & Noodle Casserole

Why You'll Love It:
A cheesy, beefy pasta bake that's rich, creamy, and super satisfying!

Ingredients

1 lb ground beef

12 oz egg noodles

1 can (10 oz) cream of mushroom soup

1 cup sour cream

1 cup shredded cheddar cheese

Instructions

1. Preheat Oven

Set to 375°F (190°C).

2. Cook the Pasta & Beef

Boil egg noodles until al dente. Drain.

Brown ground beef in a pan, then drain excess grease.

3. Assemble the Casserole

In a baking dish, mix beef, noodles, soup, sour cream, and half the cheese.

Sprinkle remaining cheese on top.

4. Bake & Serve

Bake for 25 minutes, until cheese is bubbly.

Serves: 6-8

CHAPTER 7: VEGETARIAN FAVORITES

Introduction to Vegetarian Favorites

Whether you're looking to eat more plant-based meals or need vegetarian options for your family, this chapter is filled with hearty, protein-packed meals that are full of flavor and simple to make.

Each recipe in this chapter:
- ✅ Uses eggs, dairy, and fish (no meat)
- ✅ Is hearty, filling, and satisfying
- ✅ Features easy, affordable ingredients

Let's dig into these 15 delicious vegetarian recipes!

1. Creamy Tomato Basil Soup with Grilled Cheese

Why You'll Love It:
This rich, comforting tomato soup pairs perfectly with a golden, crispy grilled cheese sandwich—a timeless favorite!

Ingredients

1 can (28 oz) crushed tomatoes

2 cups vegetable broth

1 cup heavy cream

2 tbsp butter

1 tsp dried basil

For the Grilled Cheese:

8 slices bread

4 slices cheddar cheese

2 tbsp butter

Instructions

1. Make the Soup

In a pot, melt butter, then add crushed tomatoes, broth, and basil.

Simmer for 15 minutes, then stir in heavy cream.

2. Make the Grilled Cheese

Butter one side of each slice of bread.

Place cheese between two slices and grill in a pan for 3 minutes per side.

3. Serve & Enjoy

Ladle soup into bowls and serve with grilled cheese!

Serves: 4-6

2. Vegetarian Chili

Why You'll Love It:
A hearty, flavorful chili packed with beans, tomatoes, and warm spices—perfect for a cozy meal!

Ingredients

- 1 can (15 oz) black beans
- 1 can (15 oz) kidney beans
- 1 can (28 oz) crushed tomatoes
- 1 small onion (diced)
- 1 tbsp chili powder

Instructions

1. Sauté the Onion

In a pot, cook onion over medium heat for 3 minutes.

2. Add Beans & Simmer

Stir in beans, tomatoes, and chili powder.

Simmer for 20 minutes, stirring occasionally.

3. Serve Warm

Enjoy with cheese, sour cream, or cornbread!

Serves: 6

3. Caprese Pasta Salad

Why You'll Love It:
A light and fresh pasta dish with juicy tomatoes, mozzarella, and basil, perfect as a side dish or main course.

Ingredients

12 oz pasta (penne or rotini)

1 cup cherry tomatoes (halved)

1 cup fresh mozzarella (cubed or pearls)

½ cup fresh basil (chopped)

2 tbsp olive oil

1 tbsp balsamic vinegar

½ tsp salt

½ tsp black pepper

Instructions

1. Cook the Pasta

Boil pasta in salted water until al dente. Drain and let cool.

2. Toss the Salad

In a large bowl, mix pasta, cherry tomatoes, mozzarella, and basil.

Drizzle with olive oil and balsamic vinegar.

3. Season & Serve

Toss everything together and season with salt and pepper.

Refrigerate for 30 minutes before serving for best flavor.

Serves: 6

4. Spinach & Feta Stuffed Peppers

Why You'll Love It:
A nutritious, cheesy dish featuring roasted bell peppers filled with a spinach and feta mixture.

Ingredients

4 bell peppers (halved and deseeded)

2 cups fresh spinach (chopped)

1 cup feta cheese (crumbled)

½ cup cooked quinoa or rice

1 tbsp olive oil

½ tsp garlic powder

Instructions

1. Preheat Oven

Set to 375°F (190°C).

2. Prepare the Filling

In a pan, sauté spinach in olive oil for 2 minutes, until wilted.

Mix with feta cheese, quinoa, and garlic powder.

3. Stuff the Peppers

Fill bell pepper halves with the spinach mixture.

4. Bake & Serve

Place in a baking dish and bake for 20 minutes, until peppers are tender.

Serves: 4

5. Lemon Garlic Butter Salmon

Why You'll Love It:
A rich, flaky salmon dish infused with buttery lemon garlic sauce, ready in minutes!

Ingredients

4 salmon fillets

2 tbsp butter (melted)

2 cloves garlic (minced)

2 tbsp lemon juice

½ tsp black pepper

Instructions

1. Preheat Oven

Set to 400°F (200°C).

2. Prepare the Salmon

Place salmon fillets on a lined baking sheet.

Brush with butter, garlic, and lemon juice.

Sprinkle with black pepper.

3. Bake & Serve

Bake for 12-15 minutes, until salmon flakes easily.

Serves: 4

6. Broccoli & Cheese Quiche

Why You'll Love It:
A fluffy, savory egg dish packed with broccoli and melty cheese, perfect for breakfast or dinner.

Ingredients

1 pie crust (store-bought or homemade)

1 cup broccoli (chopped & steamed)

1 cup shredded cheddar cheese

4 eggs

1 cup milk

½ tsp salt

Instructions

1. Preheat Oven

Set to 375°F (190°C).

2. Prepare the Filling

In a bowl, whisk eggs, milk, and salt.

Stir in broccoli and cheese.

3. Assemble & Bake

Pour mixture into pie crust.

Bake for 35 minutes, until the center is set.

Serves: 6

7. Vegetable Stir-Fry with Tofu

Why You'll Love It:
A colorful, protein-packed stir-fry with crispy tofu and fresh vegetables.

Ingredients

1 block firm tofu (cubed)

1 tbsp soy sauce

1 tbsp cornstarch

2 tbsp vegetable oil

2 cups mixed vegetables (bell peppers, carrots, broccoli)

1 tsp ginger (grated)

Instructions

1. Crisp the Tofu

Toss tofu cubes with cornstarch and soy sauce.

Sauté in oil over medium heat until golden brown.

2. Cook the Vegetables

Stir-fry vegetables and ginger for 5 minutes.

3. Combine & Serve

Mix in crispy tofu and serve with rice or noodles.

Serves: 4

8. Mushroom Risotto

Why You'll Love It:
A creamy, slow-cooked rice dish with rich, umami-packed mushrooms, making it the perfect vegetarian comfort food.

Ingredients

1 ½ cups Arborio rice

4 cups vegetable broth (heated)

1 cup mushrooms (sliced)

½ cup Parmesan cheese (grated)

½ cup white wine (optional, can substitute extra broth)

1 tbsp butter

1 tbsp olive oil

1 small onion (diced)

2 cloves garlic (minced)

Instructions

1. Sauté the Aromatics

Heat butter and olive oil in a pan over medium heat.

Add onion, garlic, and mushrooms, and cook for 5 minutes until softened.

2. Toast the Rice

Stir in Arborio rice and cook for 2 minutes, stirring constantly.

Pour in white wine (if using) and let it absorb.

3. Slowly Add Broth

Add ½ cup vegetable broth at a time, stirring continuously until absorbed.

Repeat until all broth is used and rice is creamy and tender (about 20 minutes).

4. Finish with Cheese & Serve

Stir in Parmesan cheese, then serve warm.

Serves: 4-6

9. Sweet Potato & Black Bean Tacos

Why You'll Love It:
A hearty, delicious vegetarian taco filling packed with roasted sweet potatoes, black beans, and bold spices.

Ingredients

2 medium sweet potatoes (peeled & diced)

1 can (15 oz) black beans (drained)

1 tbsp olive oil

1 tsp chili powder

½ tsp cumin

8 corn tortillas

½ cup sour cream (for serving, optional)

Instructions

1. Roast the Sweet Potatoes

Preheat oven to 400°F (200°C).

Toss sweet potatoes with olive oil, chili powder, and cumin.

Spread on a baking sheet and roast for 25 minutes, until tender.

2. Warm the Beans

In a pan, heat black beans over low heat for 5 minutes.

3. Assemble the Tacos

Fill corn tortillas with roasted sweet potatoes and black beans.

4. Serve & Enjoy

Top with sour cream, salsa, or avocado.

Serves: 4

10. Baked Eggplant Parmesan

Why You'll Love It:
A vegetarian twist on a classic Italian favorite—crispy, baked eggplant slices layered with marinara and melted cheese.

Ingredients

1 large eggplant (sliced into rounds)

1 cup breadcrumbs

½ cup Parmesan cheese (grated)

1 tsp Italian seasoning

2 cups marinara sauce

1 ½ cups shredded mozzarella cheese

2 eggs (beaten)

Instructions

1. Preheat Oven

Set to 375°F (190°C).

2. Bread the Eggplant

Mix breadcrumbs, Parmesan, and Italian seasoning in a bowl.

Dip eggplant slices into beaten eggs, then coat in the breadcrumb mixture.

3. Bake the Eggplant

Place on a baking sheet and bake for 20 minutes, flipping halfway.

4. Assemble & Bake Again

Spread marinara sauce in a baking dish, layer with baked eggplant and mozzarella cheese.

Repeat layers, ending with cheese on top.

Bake for 15 more minutes until cheese is bubbly.

Serves: 6

11. Lentil Soup

Why You'll Love It:
A hearty, protein-rich soup that's simple, comforting, and budget-friendly.

Ingredients

1 cup brown lentils (rinsed)

1 small onion (diced)

2 carrots (chopped)

4 cups vegetable broth

1 can (14 oz) diced tomatoes

1 tsp cumin

½ tsp salt

Instructions

1. Sauté the Aromatics

In a pot, cook onion and carrots over medium heat for 5 minutes.

2. Add Lentils & Broth

Stir in lentils, diced tomatoes, broth, cumin, and salt.

3. Simmer & Serve

Bring to a boil, then reduce heat and simmer for 30 minutes, until lentils are tender.

Serves: 6

12. Zucchini Fritters

Why You'll Love It:
These crispy, golden fritters are savory and packed with flavor—perfect as a side or snack.

Ingredients

2 medium zucchinis (grated & squeezed dry)

½ cup flour

1 egg

¼ cup Parmesan cheese

½ tsp salt

½ tsp black pepper

2 tbsp olive oil

Instructions

1. Prepare the Batter

In a bowl, mix zucchini, flour, egg, Parmesan, salt, and pepper.

2. Cook the Fritters

Heat olive oil in a pan over medium heat.

Scoop spoonfuls of batter into the pan, pressing down slightly.

Cook for 3 minutes per side, until golden brown.

3. Serve & Enjoy

Serve warm with sour cream or yogurt dip.

Serves: 4

13. Garlic Butter Shrimp Pasta

Why You'll Love It:
This light, flavorful seafood pasta dish is packed with garlicky, buttery shrimp and can be made in under 30 minutes!

Ingredients

12 oz spaghetti or linguine

1 lb shrimp (peeled & deveined)

3 tbsp butter

4 cloves garlic (minced)

½ cup Parmesan cheese (grated)

½ tsp red pepper flakes (optional)

1 tbsp lemon juice

½ tsp salt

½ tsp black pepper

Instructions

1. Cook the Pasta

Boil spaghetti in salted water until al dente. Drain and set aside.

2. Sauté the Shrimp

In a large skillet, melt butter over medium heat.

Add garlic and red pepper flakes; cook for 1 minute.

Add shrimp, salt, and pepper, cooking for 2-3 minutes per side until pink.

3. Combine Everything

Toss in the cooked pasta, lemon juice, and Parmesan cheese.

Stir well and cook for 1-2 minutes until combined.

4. Serve & Enjoy

Serve warm, garnished with extra Parmesan and fresh parsley.

Serves: 4

14. Spinach & Ricotta Stuffed Shells

Why You'll Love It:
A cheesy, baked pasta dish featuring creamy ricotta, spinach, and marinara sauce, perfect for a hearty and comforting meal.

Ingredients

12 jumbo pasta shells

2 cups ricotta cheese

1 cup shredded mozzarella cheese

1 cup fresh spinach (chopped & sautéed)

1 egg

½ tsp garlic powder

2 cups marinara sauce

½ cup Parmesan cheese (grated)

Instructions

1. Preheat Oven
Set to 375°F (190°C).

2. Cook the Pasta
Boil jumbo shells until al dente, then drain and set aside.

3. Prepare the Filling
In a bowl, mix ricotta, mozzarella, sautéed spinach, egg, and garlic powder.

4. Assemble the Dish
Spread 1 cup marinara sauce in a baking dish.
Fill each shell with the ricotta mixture and place in the dish.
Pour the remaining marinara sauce over the top and sprinkle with Parmesan cheese.

5. Bake & Serve
Cover with foil and bake for 20 minutes.
Remove foil and bake for 5 more minutes, until bubbly.

Serves: 6

15. Mediterranean Chickpea Salad

Why You'll Love It:
This light, refreshing, and protein-packed salad is loaded with chickpeas, feta, and olives, making it a perfect meal or side dish.

Ingredients

1 can (15 oz) chickpeas (drained & rinsed)

1 cup cherry tomatoes (halved)

½ cup cucumber (diced)

¼ cup red onion (thinly sliced)

¼ cup feta cheese (crumbled)

¼ cup kalamata olives (sliced)

2 tbsp olive oil

1 tbsp lemon juice

½ tsp oregano

½ tsp salt

½ tsp black pepper

Instructions

1. Prepare the Salad

In a large bowl, combine chickpeas, cherry tomatoes, cucumber, red onion, feta, and olives.

2. Make the Dressing

In a small bowl, whisk together olive oil, lemon juice, oregano, salt, and pepper.

3. Toss & Serve

Pour the dressing over the salad and toss to combine.

Refrigerate for 15 minutes before serving for the best flavor.

Serves: 4-6

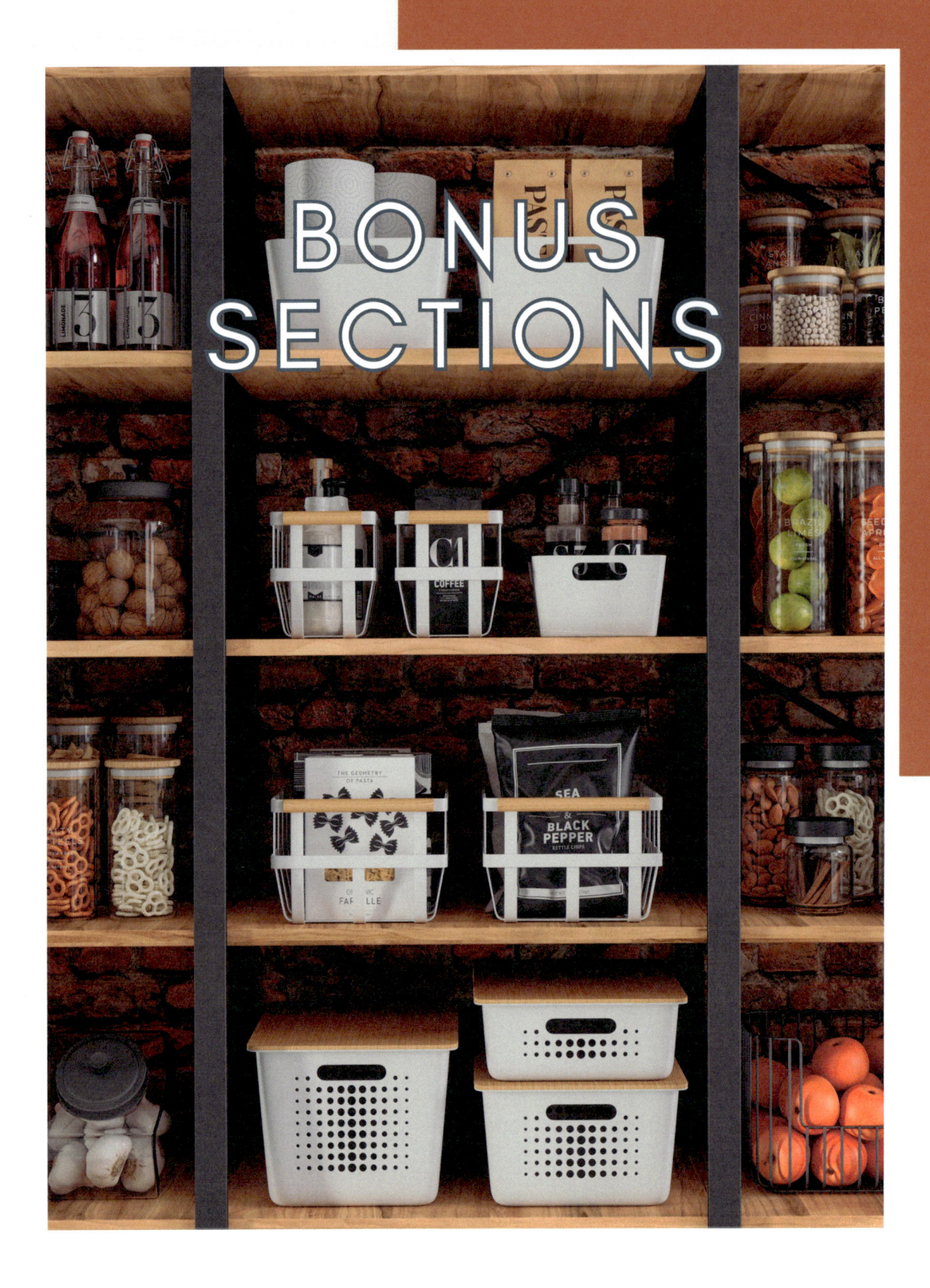

BONUS SECTIONS

Bonus Section 1: Pantry Staples for Large Families

(Stock your kitchen with essentials to make mealtime easier and more affordable!)

Feeding a large family means always having a well-stocked pantry with ingredients that are versatile, affordable, and long-lasting. Here are my go-to pantry staples that help me create fast, delicious meals without breaking the bank.

🥦 Dry Goods & Grains

✔ Rice (white, brown, or jasmine)
✔ Pasta (spaghetti, penne, macaroni)
✔ Dried or canned beans (black, kidney, pinto, chickpeas)
✔ Lentils (great for soups & veggie burgers)
✔ Oats (for breakfast and baking)
✔ Flour (all-purpose, whole wheat)
✔ Cornmeal (for cornbread, polenta)
✔ Bread crumbs (for coating meats & casseroles)

🥫 Canned & Jarred Goods

✔ Canned tomatoes (diced, crushed, paste)
✔ Canned vegetables (corn, green beans, peas)
✔ Canned tuna & salmon
✔ Canned coconut milk (for curries)
✔ Peanut butter (protein-packed & kid-friendly)
✔ Pasta sauce (for quick meals)
✔ Broths & stocks (chicken, beef, vegetable)

🫙 Oils, Sauces & Condiments

✔ Olive oil & vegetable oil
✔ Soy sauce & Worcestershire sauce
✔ Hot sauce (for extra flavor!)
✔ Vinegar (white, apple cider, balsamic)
✔ Mustard & ketchup
✔ Honey & maple syrup
✔ Ranch dressing & mayonnaise

🧂 Spices & Seasonings (Flavor makes everything better!)

✔ Salt & black pepper
✔ Garlic powder & onion powder
✔ Italian seasoning & oregano
✔ Paprika & chili powder
✔ Cumin & turmeric
✔ Cinnamon & nutmeg
✔ Bay leaves (for soups & stews)

🥚 Fresh & Refrigerated Essentials

✔ Eggs (a protein-packed staple)
✔ Cheese (cheddar, mozzarella, Parmesan)
✔ Milk (or non-dairy alternatives)
✔ Yogurt (great for breakfasts & sauces)
✔ Butter & margarine
✔ Fresh vegetables (potatoes, onions, carrots)

Bonus Section 2: Time-Saving Kitchen Hacks for Large Families

(Make cooking easier with these time-saving tricks!)

1 Meal Prep Like a Pro

- Chop veggies in advance – Store them in airtight containers in the fridge for quick meals.
- Pre-cook proteins – Cook and shred chicken or brown ground beef ahead of time for easy meals.
- Double recipes & freeze half – Soups, casseroles, and pasta sauces freeze beautifully!

2 Make the Most of Your Freezer

- Freeze leftovers in portioned bags – Perfect for quick meals on busy nights.
- Use muffin tins for freezing sauces – Great for freezing small portions of pasta sauce or soup.
- Keep frozen veggies on hand – They cook fast and eliminate chopping time.

3 Cook Once, Eat Twice

- Turn roasted chicken into multiple meals – Tacos, sandwiches, casseroles!
- Leftover pasta becomes a pasta bake – Just add cheese and bake.
- Rice leftovers make the best fried rice – Just add veggies and an egg.

4 One-Pot & Sheet Pan Meals = Less Cleaning

- Instant Pot & slow cooker meals save time – Dump everything in and let it cook.
- Sheet pan dinners = easy clean-up – Toss everything on a pan and roast together.

Bonus Section 3: Money-Saving Grocery Shopping Tips

(Stretch your grocery budget without sacrificing flavor!)

1 Buy in Bulk (But Only What You'll Use!)

- Stock up on rice, beans, pasta, and flour in bulk.
- Buy family packs of meat and freeze portions for later.
- Get spices in bulk – Cheaper and lasts longer!

2 Plan Your Meals & Make a List

- Plan weekly meals based on what's on sale.
- Stick to your list – No impulse buys!
- Use store apps & coupons for extra savings.

3 Cook From Scratch When Possible

- Homemade bread, pizza dough, and snacks save money & taste better.
- Make your own seasoning blends instead of buying pre-made packets.

📌 Bonus Section 4: Leftover Transformations

(Turn Tonight's Meal into Tomorrow's Lunch!)
One of the best ways to save time and money in the kitchen is to repurpose leftovers into new, delicious meals. Instead of eating the same thing twice, use these smart tricks to turn leftovers into something fresh and exciting!

🍗 Leftover Chicken: New Meal Ideas
- Shred rotisserie or baked chicken for tacos, enchiladas, or wraps.
- Add to pasta dishes like Alfredo or a creamy chicken & rice casserole.
- Toss into a salad for a protein-packed lunch.
- Make chicken salad with mayo, celery, and seasonings for sandwiches.

Example: Rotisserie Chicken → BBQ Chicken Sliders

1️⃣ Shred leftover chicken and mix with BBQ sauce.
2️⃣ Spoon onto Hawaiian rolls with cheese.
3️⃣ Bake at 350°F for 10 minutes for melty goodness!

🥩 Leftover Ground Beef: New Meal Ideas
- Turn leftover taco meat into a burrito bowl with rice & beans.
- Use seasoned ground beef for stuffed peppers or a taco salad.
- Stir into pasta sauce for a quick spaghetti Bolognese.
- Layer into a casserole with cheese and tortillas for beef enchiladas.

Example: Leftover Taco Meat → Cheesy Taco Pasta

1️⃣ Cook pasta, drain, and return to the pot.
2️⃣ Stir in taco meat, a splash of salsa, and shredded cheese.
3️⃣ Simmer until cheese is melted. Serve hot!

🥔 Leftover Mashed Potatoes: New Meal Ideas
- Mix into dough for potato pancakes or fritters.
- Use as a topping for Shepherd's Pie.
- Stir into soups for a creamy texture.
- Form into cheesy mashed potato balls and bake or fry!

Example: Leftover Mashed Potatoes → Cheesy Potato Pancakes

1. Mix 1 cup mashed potatoes with ¼ cup shredded cheese and an egg.
2. Form into patties and pan-fry in butter until crispy.
3. Serve with sour cream!

🍞 Leftover Bread: New Meal Ideas
- Make homemade croutons – Cube and bake with olive oil & garlic.
- Use for French toast the next morning.
- Blend into bread crumbs for coating chicken or fish.
- Layer into an easy bread pudding for dessert!

Example: Leftover Bread → Garlic Parmesan Croutons

1. Cube day-old bread and toss with olive oil, garlic powder, and Parmesan.
2. Bake at 375°F for 10-12 minutes until crispy.
3. Add to soups & salads!

📌 Bonus Section 5: Freezer Meal Guide

(The Best Meals to Prep & Freeze for Busy Nights!)

Freezer meals are lifesavers for busy families! By prepping meals ahead of time, you can save money, reduce food waste, and always have dinner ready to go.

📌 Best Freezer-Friendly Meals
- ☑ Soups & Stews – Chili, beef stew, chicken noodle soup.
- ☑ Casseroles – Baked ziti, lasagna, enchiladas, mac & cheese.
- ☑ Marinated Meats – Chicken, beef, and pork with sauce in freezer bags.
- ☑ Breakfast Items – Pancakes, waffles, egg muffins.
- ☑ Slow Cooker Meals – Pre-chopped ingredients frozen in a bag, ready to dump & cook.

📌 How to Freeze & Reheat Meals Properly

Freezing Tips
- ✔ Cool food completely before freezing.
- ✔ Store in airtight containers or freezer bags.
- ✔ Label each item with the date & reheating instructions.
- ✔ Use freezer-friendly glass or plastic containers for soups & sauces.

Reheating Tips
- ✔ For casseroles – Thaw overnight, then bake at 350°F for 25-30 minutes.
- ✔ For soups – Reheat on the stovetop over medium heat, adding broth if needed.
- ✔ For meats – Thaw in the fridge overnight, then cook as usual.

📌 Bonus Section 6: Batch Cooking for Large Families

(How to Cook Once & Eat Twice!)

Batch cooking means preparing large portions of food at once so you can serve multiple meals with minimal extra effort. This is a game-changer for large families!

📌 Best Foods for Batch Cooking
- ✔ **Proteins** – Ground beef, shredded chicken, pulled pork.
- ✔ **Grains** – Rice, quinoa, pasta.
- ✔ **Soups & Stews** – Chili, beef stew, vegetable soup.
- ✔ **Sauces** – Marinara, Alfredo, taco meat.
- ✔ **Breakfast Items** – Pancakes, muffins, egg casseroles.

📌 How to Batch Cook Efficiently
- ◆ **Pick a cooking day** – Choose one day a week to cook in bulk.
- ◆ **Use multiple appliances** – Slow cooker, Instant Pot, and oven at the same time.
- ◆ **Freeze in portions** – Store meals in family-sized or single-portion servings.
- ◆ **Prep ingredients in advance** – Chop all veggies, marinate meats, and portion everything before cooking.

📌 Example Batch Cooking Plan for a Week
- ✔ **Day 1:** Cook 3 lbs of ground beef – Use for tacos, pasta, and sloppy joes.
- ✔ **Day 2:** Roast two whole chickens – Use for salads, wraps, casseroles, and soup.
- ✔ **Day 3:** Make a big pot of rice – Use for stir-fry, burrito bowls, and fried rice.
- ✔ **Day 4:** Prepare marinated meats for the freezer – Ready for quick meals later.

💛 A Note from Me to You

Wow! You made it to the end of Mom of 10's Complete Cookbook—I hope this book fills your kitchen with delicious meals, warm memories, and joyful moments shared around the table.

Cooking for a family, whether big or small, isn't just about feeding mouths—it's about nourishing hearts. It's about laughing together over spilled milk, finding ways to make leftovers exciting, and knowing that even on the busiest, messiest, and most exhausting days… you did something amazing just by putting food on the table.

I know how overwhelming it can feel to meal plan, budget groceries, and cook daily—but you're doing it. And that's something to be proud of! Whether you made a quick 30-minute meal on a chaotic weekday or served up a comforting family favorite on a Sunday night, every effort you make is worth it.
So when you're tired, when the dishes pile up, when you feel like you're running on empty—remember this:

👉 You are doing an incredible job.
👉 Your family appreciates you, even if they don't always say it.
👉 Every meal you make is an act of love.

I hope this cookbook has helped make mealtime easier, budget-friendlier, and more enjoyable for you and your family.

Thank you for letting me be a part of your kitchen.
If you loved this cookbook, I'd love to hear from you! Reviews, messages, and even photos of your family enjoying these meals mean the world to me. 💛

From my home to yours,
Karla

Want More Recipes & Tips?
📍 Follow me for more: @thebradleybunchadventures
📍 Leave a review on Amazon – Your feedback helps me create even more great content!
📍 Tag me in your meals! – I'd love to see what you're cooking!
🍴 Happy Cooking & Happy Eating! 🍴

Mom of 10's Complete Cookbook: Fast, Easy, and Budget-Friendly Recipes

Feeding a big family on a budget doesn't have to be overwhelming! In this cookbook, Karla Bradley, a mom of 10, shares her tried-and-true recipes that are:

✓ Fast & Easy – Most meals are ready in 30 minutes or less or use the Instant Pot for extra convenience.
✓ Budget-Friendly – Delicious, home-cooked meals for $3 per person or less.
✓ Family-Approved – Recipes tested and loved by kids and adults alike!
✓ Crowd-Pleasing – Perfect for large families, potlucks, and gatherings.

From one-pot wonders and 5-ingredient meals to comfort food classics and vegetarian favorites, this book has over 100 easy recipes designed to help busy parents feed their families without stress.

If you're looking for delicious, budget-friendly meals that even picky eaters will love, this is the cookbook for you!

Inside, you'll find:
✓ 7 easy-to-follow recipe categories for every occasion
✓ Time-saving meal prep & grocery shopping tips
✓ Money-saving hacks for feeding a large family

Get ready to spend less time in the kitchen and more time enjoying meals with your family!